Paul Valéry

(*TWAS 43*)

Paul Valéry

By HENRY A. GRUBBS

Oberlin College

Twayne Publishers, Inc.   ::   New York

To
MIREILLE

Preface

The aim of this book is to give the American reader as complete a picture as is possible—within the scope of a relatively short volume—of the great French writer, Paul Valéry. Excellent biographies of Valéry, as well as general and specialized studies of his work, are available in French (though two of the best, those by Maurice Bémol and Pierre-Olivier Walzer—see Bibliography—are now out of print), but there is only one general study in English, that by Agnes Mackay (oddly titled: *The Universal Self*). Francis Scarfe's fine *Art of Paul Valéry* (also out of print) is really a thesis, and hence limited in scope.

Although it is probably too early to make a definitive judgment of Valéry's final place in French literature, it is now possible to present a rather complete picture of his life and work. In the last ten to fifteen years, in addition to a number of studies, based upon manuscripts and variants, of the poet's methods of poetic composition, much of the correspondence has been published, and, most valuable of all for an understanding of this complex man, we now have a photographic reproduction of the *cahiers*, Valéry's daily notes, preserved in no less than 257 little notebooks. These publications have furnished much hitherto unknown material, of which, I trust, I have made judicious use.

After a "chronology," listing by dates the main events in Valéry's life, I have told, in more detail, in four chapters, the story of that life, stressing those features which were most related to his work, both the poetry and the prose. This is an unusual life: a great poet, who disliked being called a poet, a master of modern thought who had a horror of being called "maître," one of the great French writers of the early twentieth century who avoided the career of a literary man until the age of fifty and then accepted such a career for practical reasons only (to make a living for his family). I have endeavored to bring into focus these anomalies of Paul Valéry, in whom we may see in turn the figures of Narcissus and Orpheus . . . and also of Leonardo da Vinci.

My biography of Valéry is in no way a duplication of that given by the poet's daughter, Agathe Rouart-Valéry, in the introduction to the easily available, if expensive, Pléiade edition of the poet's works: that is a detailed account (sixty pages of fine print) of Valéry's activities, day by day, year by year. Since many of these activities had little relation to what interests us most here—the poetry, the important prose writings, the thought —I have not attempted to list Valéry's trips to the Riviera in the summer, his participation in official ceremonies, his lectures in Zurich or in Milan, etc.

I have always found Valéry's poetical theory of great interest, and hence I have discussed this in some detail in my fifth chapter. In a sixth chapter I have attempted something more difficult: to estimate Valéry's ranks and lasting importance as a poet. A final chapter discusses his thought, and, incidentally, his prose writings.

My bibliography is of necessity highly selective. I have tried to make it useful by giving my own estimate of the value and the interest of the works listed. I have read all books and articles mentioned, with the exception of one of each.

I resisted the temptation to quote freely from the poetry. This would have involved extensive translation, and the few attempts at translation that I made seemed to me rather unsatisfactory. The poetry of Valéry is easily available; Gallimard has recently issued it as a paperback in its new poetry series. Excellent (though often widely divergent) exegeses of most of the poems exist, and I have listed the best of these in my Bibliography.

The poetry quoted is followed by my own literal translations: what Mallarmé called *calques* (tracings). The prose quotations are given in English, in my own translations. Here I aimed not at a *calque*, but at as accurate (if often free) rendering of the *meaning* as was possible.

I wish to thank the Librairie Gallimard for their generous permission to quote several poems complete.

HENRY A. GRUBBS

Oberlin, Ohio
August, 1966

Contents

PAUL VALERY

by

HENRY A. GRUBBS

This is the first book in English on Paul Valery for the general reader. Four chapters relate the poet's life, stressing his intellectual and poetic development. Mr. Grubbs evokes the mythical figures of Orpheus, symbolizing artistic creation, and Narcissus, symbolizing the completely disinterested cultivation of one's own mind, as an interpretation of the changes in direction made by Paul Valéry in his relatively long and very active life. This book is intended to be accessible to readers who know no French; therefore all quotations have been translated, and since translations of Valéry's poetry into English prose give little hint of the beauty of the original, these are limited in number.

After the biographical section, successive chapters are devoted to the poet's paradoxical poetics (treated *in extenso* in two previous books, but without the complete knowledge of those theories afforded by the publication of Valéry's 250 and more intimate notebooks), to Valéry's rank and lasting importance as a poet, and finally his position as a thinker. This last chapter involves a complete study of the extremely varied prose writings.

In addition to the usual notes and references, there is a highly selective, up-to-date and annotated bibliography and an index

Chronology

1871 Paul-Ambroise Valéry is born October 30 in the city of Sète (then spelled Cette) on the western Mediterranean coast of France. His father, Barthélemy Valéry, was a Corsican, his mother, Fanny Grassi, Italian.

1878 He goes to school at the Collège de Sète (now called Collège Paul-Valéry).

1884 The family moves to Montpellier, where Valéry enters the Lycée (which he dislikes), and he begins to write poetry.

1887 Valéry's father dies. (His mother is to live 40 years longer.)

1888 After completing his *baccalauréat*, Valéry enters the law school of the University of Montpellier.

1889 A reading of Huysmans' novel *A Rebours* introduces him to the poetry of Mallarmé, for him a great discovery. In November he interrupts his studies for a year of military service.

1890 On the occasion of the celebration of the sixth centenary of the University, Valéry makes the acquaintance of a young Parisian, Pierre Louÿs, and through him becomes friends with André Gide. The latter is to be a lifelong friendship. Poems of Valéry begin to be published in little reviews, in Paris as well as in the provinces.

1891 *La Conque*, little review founded by Pierre Louÿs, publishes "Narcisse parle" and "La Fileuse." The first of these receives considerable praise, which seems exaggerated to Valéry. First trip to Paris and meeting with Mallarmé.

1892   Receives law degree (*licence en droit*). During the "night of Genoa" (October 4–5?) an intellectual crisis comes to a head. Valéry, who had written hundreds of poems (mainly sonnets) in the three previous years, decides to renounce literature and devote himself primarily to the cultivation of his mind.

1894   In March Valéry settles definitively in Paris (he has a small room in the Hôtel Henri IV, 12, rue Gay-Lussac). He becomes a regular visitor to Mallarmé's Tuesday evenings. He also begins devoting early morning hours to noting down his thoughts in small notebooks. This activity, which he considered very important, resulted eventually in the more than 250 *cahiers*.

1895   *Introduction à la méthode de Léonard de Vinci* is published in the *Nouvelle Revue*. Feeling the need of a regular job, a means of earning his living, Valéry takes examination for entry into the War Office. He is accepted, but not actually appointed until May 1897.

1896   *La Soirée avec Monsieur Teste* is published in *Le Centaure*.

1898   Valéry is deeply moved by the death of Mallarmé, to whom he had become attached. He meets Jeannie Gobillard, niece of the painter Berthe Morisot and friend of Mallarmé's daughter.

1900   Valéry marries Jeannie Gobillard. He leaves the War Office and becomes private secretary of Edouard Lebey, director of the French press association, the Agence Havas. The important anthology of poetry, *Poètes d'aujourd'hui*, edited by Van Bever and Léautaud, publishes a representative selection of Valéry's early poems. This keeps his work from being forgotten.

1902   Valéry moves to an apartment, 40, rue de Villejust (now rue Paul-Valéry), where he was to live for the rest of his life.

1909   The newly-founded *Nouvelle Revue française* (sponsored by Gide) publishes Valéry's essay on dreams, "Etudes."

1912   Gide and his associate, the publisher Gallimard, attempt to persuade Valéry to let them publish a volume of his early poetry and prose. Valéry reluctantly accepts and begins revising his early poems. He also begins writing a poem inspired by the recitatives of Gluck. This eventually becomes *La Jeune Parque.*

1915 Republication of "Une Conquête méthodique" (first published as "La Conquête allemande" in 1897, in an English review). In wartime, eighteen years later, Valéry appears to have been a remarkable prophet.

1917 Publication of *La Jeune Parque.* Surprising success of this obscure poem. Valéry is now recognized as a great poet. During the next three to four years he publishes in various reviews (including the surrealist review, *Littérature:* Valéry and André Breton were close friends for a number of years) the poems that are to constitute the collection *Charmes.*

1920 Publication of "Le Cimetière marin" in the *Nouvelle Revue française.* The best-known of Valéry's poems, it seems to be the typical obscure modern poem. Publication of early poems (most of them extensively revised) in the *Album de vers anciens.*

1921 Valéry writes and publishes his first dialogues: *Eupalinos ou l'architecte* and *L'Ame et la danse.*

1922 Publication of *Charmes* (subtitled "ou poèmes") containing the poems written 1917–1921. Death of Edouard Lebey. Now without a job, Valéry follows the advice of friends (his publisher Gallimard and two wealthy ladies interested in literature and art, Nathalie Barney and Princess Bassiano) and capitalizes on his growing reputation; makes a good living by constant writing, publishing (innumerable prefaces, deluxe editions of poems and extracts from his notebooks), and lecturing all over Europe.

1924 Publication of *Variété,* first volume of his collected essays (there were to be five in all). Becomes, with Valry Larbaud and Léon-Paul Fargue, co-editor of *Commerce,* a literary review subsidized by Princess Bassiano (1924–1932). Begins publication of extracts from his *cahiers* with *Cahier B 1910.*

1925 Elected to the Académie française in November.

1926 Publication of *Rhumbs,* another small volume of extracts from *cahiers,* to be followed in succeeding years by half a dozen more.

1927   In his speech of reception into the Académie française, Valéry surprises his audience by criticizing (without ever mentioning his name) instead of eulogizing his predecessor, Anatole France.

1928   Valéry is present at the Sorbonne when Gustave Cohen begins the course on the "Cimetière marin." His reaction is a complex of embarrassment, amusement, and admiration.

1931   Valéry gives the welcoming speech for Maréchal Pétain at the Académie. The opera produces his "mélodrame" (the name he gave to this type of ballet), *Amphion,* with music by Honegger.

1932   Publication of the dialogue *L'Idée fixe.*

1933   Valéry is named administrator of the newly created Centre Universitaire Méditerranéen at Nice.

1934   The opera produces *Sémiramis,* another "mélodrame," again with music by Honegger.

1937   Named holder of the newly created chair of poetics at the Collège de France, Valéry gives his first lecture in December. He continues giving this poetry course every winter until shortly before his death.

1940   With war and occupation, Valéry moves to Dinard, where he begins writing *Mon Faust* (published in 1941). In September he returns to Paris and remains there for most of the rest of the War.

1941   After Bergson's death, Valéry eulogizes him before the Académie. This is held to be a courageous act of resistance.

1944   Valéry's last important lecture is his *Discours sur Voltaire* in December at the Sorbonne.

1945   The poet's final illness begins toward the end of May. He dies July 20, and at the funeral services, July 24–25, he receives national honors. He is buried in the *Cimetière marin* of Sète.

CHAPTER 1

Orpheus or Narcissus?

I *A Childhood by the Sea*

PAUL VALÉRY was born October 30, 1871 [1] in the small city of Sète,[2] on the Languedoc-Mediterranean coast of France. He was baptized Ambroise, Paul, Toussaint, Jules Valéry. In his youth, for a number of years, he signed his name Paul-Ambroise Valéry, then dropped the Ambroise. His father, Barthélemy Valéry, of Corsican origin,[3] was a customs official. His mother, Fanny Grassi, was of an Italian family that claimed direct descent from the Viscontis, who were rulers of Milan in the fourteenth and fifteenth centuries. It will thus be noted that Paul Valéry was purely Mediterranean in his origins, and, I assume—though I have not had the opportunity of verifying this—completely bilingual, as much at ease in Italian as in French. We do know that in his childhood and his youth he made frequent visits to the home of an aunt in Genoa and that as late as 1924, in Rome, he discussed the intellectual currents of the day, in Italian, with Mussolini.[4]

The city of Sète is situated on a narrow strip between the sea and the broad Etang de Thau, a salt inlet. The principal feature of the otherwise flat coastal plain is the Mont Saint-Clair, rising nearly 600 feet straight up from the sea at the western edge of the town. It is on the seaside slope of this hill that there is to be found the *Cimetière marin* (Seaside Cemetery), setting of Valéry's best-known poem, and where he was buried in July, 1945. The school to which he was sent at the age of seven and which he attended for six years, the Collège de Cette (now the Collège Paul-Valéry), is on the same slope and offers magnificent views of the "Grande Bleue," the dark-blue Mediterranean. The sea was constantly before the eyes of the child Valéry—the family house was on the quay—and the love of the sea entered deeply into his soul in those childhood years.

Details on our poet's early life are relatively few. We are told

that the first word he pronounced was *clef* (key), that at the age
of three he nearly drowned in a pool in the Public Garden of
Sète, that on a trip to London in 1878 (another aunt lived there),
he was terrified by the waxworks in the Tussaud Museum.[5]

More interesting, but subject to caution, since the poet noted
this down probably at a much later date,[6] are remarks concerning the development of his intellectual life at the ages of
nine and ten—most of his games took place in his own head:

I must have begun at the age of nine or ten to constitute a sort of
island in my head, and though I was of a social and communicating
nature, I reserved for myself more and more a very secret garden
where I cultivated the images which seemed to me completely mine
and could be nothing else than mine. (*Œuvres,* I, pp. 13–4.)

Paul Valéry began his schooling at the age of five, first, for
two years at the Dominican Convent School, then, as I said above,
at the Collège de Cette. In 1884 the family moved to the much
larger city of Montpellier, 18 miles away and a few miles from
the sea. His schoolwork at Sète had not produced in him un-
favorable reactions, but the contrary was the case when he
entered the Lycée of Montpellier in the autumn of 1884. He
was presumably a docile and certainly a moderately successful
pupil, but inwardly in violent revolt against the stereotyped
nature of his studies. Although he was to continue his studies
—*baccalauréat* in 1887, *licence en droit* in 1892—he developed
at an early age and was to maintain until the end of his life a
conviction of the uselessness and meaninglessness of degrees and
diplomas. In the year he entered the Lycée, at the age of thirteen,
one of his first poems that have been preserved is a satiric parody
of Victor Hugo's "Napoléon II," eleven rather amusing verses on
the exaggerated importance attached to the "bachot" (the bac-
calaureate degree that terminates lycée studies).[7] The facts that
when the Centre Universitaire Méditerranéen was opened at
Nice in 1934 he was appointed its administrator and that he was
professor of poetics at the Collège de France from 1937 until
his death are not contradictory: these two institutions do not
give diplomas or degrees.

Thus we have seen that Paul Valéry began to write poetry
at the age of thirteen and that he knew Victor Hugo's work well

enough to parody it. Two other poems of that year, published by Henri Mondor,[8] are relatively insignificant. He had not yet found his poetic models. He soon read not only Gautier and the Parnassians but also Baudelaire. He had not yet, however, discovered Rimbaud or Mallarmé, who were still unknown outside of a small literary coterie. The young boy had interests other than poetry. Mathematics fascinated him, in theory at least, and for many years he was to pursue the study of that science and its application to other disciplines on an amateurish and autodidactic basis; but in formal study he did not go far enough to be able to enter the Naval School. A career on the sea was his earliest vocational interest, and it was probably not a passing childish whim. His only real experience of a sailor's life was to come many years later (1925), when he went for a month's cruise on a battleship.

Another interest that began early and continued long was architecture (from *Paradoxe sur l'architecte* of 1891 to *Eupalinos ou l'architecte* of 1921). Viollet le Duc's *Dictionnaire de l'architecture,* which he found in the Public Library, was favorite reading matter during his adolescence.

Lasting friendships with youths of his own age in Montpellier were formed at this time: notably those with Pierre Féline, who lived in the building to which the Valéry's had moved in 1886 (it was 3, rue Urbain V), and whose interest in mathematics in which he was an advanced student coincided with that of Paul; and a classmate, Gustave Fourment. Valéry's correspondence with Fourment, which extended over a long period and which was published in 1957 (see Bibliography), is one of our principal sources of knowledge of Valéry's early poetry. The poems he wrote between 1887 and 1890, most of them sonnets, were copied and sent to Fourment.

II *The Discovery of Mallarmé*

The most important friendships formed by Paul Valéry in his youth came in the year 1890. In November 1889 he had interrupted his law studies to volunteer for a year of service in the Army (military service was shorter and easier for volunteers). In May 1890 he obtained leave to go to a dinner given at the nearby seaside resort of Palavas-les-Flots. This dinner was part of the celebration of the sixth centenary of the foundation of the University of Montpellier. Seated next to him at the table was a young man from Paris named Pierre Louis (who was soon to change his name, for literary purposes, to Louÿs—the *s* pronounced). Louis was a year older than Valéry, and far more knowledgeable in matters of literature than the young provincial. Paul Valéry had read Joris-Karl Huysmans' *A Rebours* six months before and had discovered the existence of Paul Verlaine and, above all, of Stéphane Mallarmé. One of the eccentricities of Des Esseintes, the refined and decadent hero of Huysmans' novel, was a great admiration for the poetry of Mallarmé, then little known, and whose work was hard to obtain in the provinces. Several passages from Mallarmé's most important works were quoted in the novel.

The discovery of Mallarmé had been an overwhelming event in Valéry's life, but he had been left unsatisfied, since he was able to come upon so little of the poet's work. Now, through Pierre Louis, he was going to be put in touch with this most important poetic movement. Louis spoke to Valéry of Mallarmé's famous Tuesdays: the meeting of friends and disciples of the great poet every Tuesday evening in the humble little apartment in the rue de Rome. Louis also spoke of a friend in Paris, two years older than he, who had an uncle in Montpellier and who frequently visited the city. The friend's name was André Gide.

It was in December of the same year that Gide came to Montpellier, and made the acquaintance of Valéry. Thus was started a friendship which was to last, with numerous ups and downs— caused primarily by the difference in the temperaments of the two men—until Valéry's death.

Encouraged by Pierre Louis, Valéry had, somewhat earlier (October 20, 1890), written to Stéphane Mallarmé asking for advice with regard to a poetic career, and enclosing two poems, "Le Jeune Prêtre" and "La Suave Agonie." The reply, very prompt (October 24), was cordial and encouraging: "My dear poet . . . the gift of subtle analogy, with the adequate music, you possess that, which is all. . . . As for advice, it is given only by solitude." [9] Was Mallarmé merely being kind? He had written encouragingly, even flatteringly, to a number of quite insignificant poets. Though not by any means without merit, these poems [10] especially the second, show that in October 1890, the nineteen-year-old poet was some way from poetic maturity. "Le Jeune Prêtre" was published almost immediately in Paris: in *La Plume*,

November 15. This periodical was running a sonnet competition, and Valéry's poem received "honorable mention," behind sonnets of Marcel Noyer, Benoni Glador, Jules Labouc, Léon Leclère, Paul Rouget, Camille Soubise and Vigné d'Octon! (None of these made a name, even as a minor poet.) That Valéry did not have too high an opinion of these early poems is shown by the fact that he did not select them to be published in his *Album de vers anciens.*

The discovery of Mallarmé was a powerful poetic stimulus to the young poet of Montpellier. Was it a desire to win the respect of Mallarmé that caused him to became a prolific versifier and also to endeavor to get his poems into print? His first poem to be published, "Rêve," in the *Revue Maritime* of Marseille, in April 1889, had been sent to the magazine by his much older brother Jules, presumably without Paul's knowledge. It was later in the same year that Valéry made his own first attempt to get poetry published. He sent a poem, "Elévation de la Lune," and a critical article, "Quelques notes sur la technique littéraire," to a Paris review, *Le Courrier libre.* The poem appeared in the October number, then the review expired. This may have discouraged Valéry, but not for long.

1891 was the year in which he began to make a certain name for himself in the literary world. More than a dozen of his poems were published, most in the short-lived review *La Conque,* founded and edited by his friend Pierre Louÿs. Other periodicals to which he contributed, between 1890 and 1892, were *L'Ermitage,* one of the better-known and longer-lasting symbolist reviews, and ephemeral provincial magazines such as *Chimère* and *La Syrinx.* At least two of the poems of 1891 were of high quality, and showed that a new and unusual talent had appeared.

If we consider publication dates, the first poem in which Paul Valéry, at the age of nineteen, was to show many of the distinctive qualities of his poetry was "Narcisse parle," which appeared in the intial number of Pierre Louÿs' little review of poetry, *La Conque,* March 15, 1891.[11] The quality that I call "valéryen"— delicate harmonies, purity and originality of imagery—appears in many of the verses of this poem, some of which the poet retained intact (or almost) in the "Fragments du Narcisse" of the twenties, which some critics consider to be his best poem. Here is a sample of "Narcisse parle":

J'entends les herbes d'or grandir dans l'ombre sainte
Et la lune perfide élève son miroir . . .
Que je déplore ton éclat fatal et pur,
Source funeste à mes larmes prédestinée . . .

                                            (*Œuvres*, I, p. 82.)

(I hear the golden grasses growing in the holy shade
And the perfidious moon lifts its mirror . . .
How I deplore your fatal and pure brilliance,
Baleful fount predestined to my tears . . .)

This moderately long (for Valéry) poem of 53 verses won immediate recognition. An article published April 7, 1891, in the *Journal des Débats*, praised it highly. Chantavoine, the critic, said "his name will hover on the lips of men." (Quoted in *Œuvres*, I, p. 18.) It is worth noting, for it is characteristic of the peculiar modesty of this unusual man (already at nineteen —and he was to remain that way) that he reacted unfavorably to this praise: "which appeared premature to me, and I suffered more from it perhaps than from many more or less atrocious criticisms addressed to me later." (Quoted in *Œuvres*, I, p. 1557.)

"Narcisse parle" was reprinted in the well-known anthology of Van Bever and Léautaud, *Poètes d'aujourd'hui* (1900). It was this republication of several of his early poems that kept him from being completely forgotten during his long "period of silence."

Whereas I consider that the formal beauty of "Narcisse parle" is its most significant aspect, the subject is also of great interest for the interpretation of Valéry's life and character. Narcissus— or the myth of Narcissus—was one of the poet's frequent if not constant preoccupations (or should I say obsessions?). Let us recall his remark that, as early as the age of nine, he began cultivating images in a secret garden of his mind. A poem of 1887 (otherwise not particularly distinctive) contains a very significant verse: "Et je jouis sans fin de mon propre cerveau. . . ." (And I take delight endlessly in my own brain.) (*Œuvres*, I, p. 1585.)

Valéry himself has told of the origin of the poem "Narcisse parle," admitting that this theme was a sort of "poetic autobiography":

This theme of *Narcissus*, which I have chosen, is a sort of poetic autobiography which requires a few explanations and indications. There

exists in Montpellier a botanical garden where I used to go very often
when I was nineteen. In a rather secluded corner of this garden, which
formerly was much wilder and more attractive, there is an arch and
in that a sort of crevice containing a marble slab, which bears three
words: PLACANDIS NARCISSAE MANIBUS (to placate the spirit
of Narcissa). That inscription had brought on reveries in me, and here,
in two words, is its story.

In 1820, at this spot, there was discovered a skeleton, and according
to certain local traditions, it was thought to be the tomb of the poet
Young. This girl, who died in Montpellier toward the end of the Eight-
eenth Century, couldn't be buried in the cemetery, since she was a
Protestant. Her father is supposed to have buried her, on a moonlit
night. The dead girl was named Narcissa. The remains that had been
found were identified as hers.

For me the name Narcissa suggested Narcissus. Then I developed
the idea of the myth of this young man, perfectly handsome or who
found himself so in his reflection. I wrote at that time the very first
Narcissus, an irregular sonnet, origin of the succeeding poems. . . .

He continues:

I wrote in two days the piece entitled "Narcisse parle," a development
of the sonnet I mentioned. But the poem didn't appear until six months
later. I would have preferred to have the time to work over the
theme. . . .

At fifty years distance this first *Narcissus* seems to me today a speci-
men of what I would probably have done in the matter of poetry if I
had continued to practice it instead of turning away from it and pur-
suing in other ways the formation of my mind. The poem remains
for me a first state, characteristic of my ideal and my abilities at that
time. . . .[12]

This seems to me a sufficiently explicit statement of the importance of the myth of Narcissus to Valéry at the age of nineteen. As for his remark about "turning away from poetry," that
is a reference to a critical point in his life which I shall consider
in detail when I have finished my examination of the poetic
accomplishment of Valéry at this period.

"La Fileuse" is the other poem of the twenty-year-old Valéry
which seems to me to contain many of the best qualities of the
mature poet. Here we do not find a theme, a myth expressing
an obsession of the poet, couched in a symbol or symbols. "La

Fileuse" is simply the word-picture of a scene, not a Parnassian
marble, but a delicate impression. The poem was revised a number of times, and some of the finest images of the final version
were not in the original; e.g., the "source vive / Qui, suspendue
au jour, délicieuse arrose / De ses pertes de fleurs le jardin de
l'oisive" (living spring / Which, suspended in the daylight, waters
deliciously / with its losses of flowers the garden of the idle
girl). (*Œuvres*, I, p. 75.) Furthermore, it contains some examples of what Noël Félici called: "the sugar candy of a Samain," [13]
that is, the pretentious affected vocabulary of the minor symbolist
poets, such as the adjective "agneline" (verse 4—replaced by
"câline" in the final version). Valéry himself, in his talk on
"Narcisse parle" quoted above, refers to the rare adjective "fu-
nérale," and says it was "one of the words of the epoch of my
youth. We often used a vocabulary rather uncertain and always
far-fetched." [14]

A recent article by J. Dubu has pointed out, very plausibly,
that the source for this poem is most likely Courbet's painting,
La Fileuse endormie, in the Musée Fabre at Montpellier. [15] In a
letter to Gide of the summer of 1891, Valéry said that the first
verse came to him in his sleep. "I made a verse while sleeping
which will be for *La Conque*, probably all alone: 'Assise la
fileuse au bleu de la croisée' (Seated the spinner at the blue of
the casement)." [16] But he continued the poem and later sent it
to Gide in an incomplete form (6 tercets only). [17]

There is of course in evidence the influence of Mallarmé, but
something more, something that revealed a new and outstanding
poetic talent. Take for instance this tercet (the form given in
La Conque was maintained in the final version):

> Une tige, où le vent vagabond se repose
> Courbe la salut vain de sa grâce étoilée
> Dédiant, magnifique, au vieux rouet, sa rose.
> (*Œuvres*, I, p. 75.)

(A stem, where the vagabond wind reposes / Bends the vain
salute of its starry grace / dedicating, magnificent, to the old
spinning wheel, its rose.)
Or these, the final verses of the poem:

Ta sœur, la grande rose où sourit une sainte
Parfume ton front vague au vent de son haleine
Innocente qui crois languir dans l'heure éteinte.[18]
(*Œuvres,* I, p. 1534.)

(Your sister, the great rose where smiles a sainted maiden /
perfumes your vague forehead with the wind of its innocent
breath / you who think you are languishing in the extinguished
hour.)

During this period of poetic activity (1890–1892), Paul Valéry
finished his military service. He then went back to the Faculté
de Droit of the University of Montpellier, where, as I mentioned
above, he obtained his *licence-en-droit* in the summer of 1892.
In September 1891 he had gone to Paris for the first time, accompanying his mother on a visit to his older brother, Jules, then an
advanced law student in Paris. They stayed a month. Valéry
made the acquaintance of Huysmans, whose *A Rebours* he
admired so much, and was taken by Louÿs to the Tuesdays of
Mallarmé. Personal acquaintance with the Master did not di-
minish the young poet's admiration: on the contrary!

III *The Crisis*

When Valéry finished his studies in July 1892, he spent a
difficult summer, marked by an unhappy love affair of which
we know little. All we are told is that Valéry fell in love with a
married woman who is partly identified as Madame "Rov." or
"de Rov" and as being of Catalan origin. In a note written nearly
fifty years later (1940) he spoke of the violence of this "absurd
affair" (he never even spoke to Madame de Rov.), from which
he suffered for several years. (*Cahiers,* vol. 23, pp. 589–590.)

In September he went to Genoa with his family, staying as
usual in the apartment of his Aunt Cabella, Salita San Francesco,
overlooking the port. The night of October 4–5[19] there was a
violent and very prolonged thunderstorm, frightening and beautiful at the same time. This, according to the majority of the
biographers of Valéry, was the occasion of the crisis which opened
the period in the poet's life known as the "Great Silence." The
rather generally accepted view is that Valéry gave up poetry
altogether for a long interval, which did not end until twenty-

five years later with the publication of *La Jeune Parque* (1917).

Valéry himself was somewhat contradictory in dating his crisis, which has been called the "Genoa night." In one of the "Personal Notes," quoted by his daughter in her biography, he spoke of a "frightful night—spent on my bed—the storm everywhere—my room dazzlingly bright with each lightning flash—and my whole fate was being decided in my head. I am between myself and myself." (*Œuvres*, I, p. 20.) He later wrote, in a letter to Guy de Pourtalès: "As for Genoa . . . I nearly became mad there in 1892. A certain *white* night—white with lightning—which I spent sitting up, and hoping that a bolt would strike me. . . . It was a question of decomposing for myself all my first ideas or idols, and breaking off from a me who couldn't do what he wanted and didn't want to do what he could." [20] These statements would definitely date the "crisis" the night of October 4–5.

But, on another occasion, he wrote to Pierre Louÿs: "I begin by recalling that all my intellectual life is dominated by the event of November 1892. Just having returned to Paris to settle down there, I was the victim of a coincidence which was the biggest of all those that had reduced me to absurdity during the years 1891–1892 and finally forced me to flee." [21] This "coincidence" was apparently a chance meeting in Paris with the innamorata of Montpellier. At least Valéry thought it was a chance meeting, in fact was not quite sure that his eyes were not deceiving him, but it seems likely that this event was contrived by one of his Montpellier friends, Charles Auzilion, who was then in Paris.[22]

The decision brought about by the crisis was to give up poetry, and literature in general, and to turn to something else. Exactly what this was to which he turned, and why he made such a decision will require detailed explanation.

First of all, the "silence" was by no means complete. How could a born poet, to whom beautiful verses like "Assise la fileuse au bleu de la croisée" came in his sleep, give up poetry completely? The fact is that at least half a dozen of the twenty-one poems of the 1920 *Album de vers anciens* were written after October 1892. These poems, which, in contrast to the poems of *youth* (1889–1892), are called poems of *majority* (1892–1900), are of uniformly high quality, and two ("Vue" and "Eté," published in the *Centaure* in 1896) are among his finest. It was after his marriage, between 1900 and 1912, that Valéry's poetic activity became nearly dormant. But, in contrast to the years immediately preceding 1892, when Valéry was very prolific, he was *relatively* inactive, poetically, during the years of the "Great Silence."

I shall note in passing the interesting and not really irrelevant fact that three French poets of the generation preceding Valéry's had experiences of a somewhat similar nature. Rimbaud's complete abandonment of poetry at the age of twenty to twenty-one is well known. Our knowledge of the life of Isidore Ducasse, "Comte de Lautréamont," is too limited to say with certainty that he turned away from poetry shortly before his untimely death, but the letters that have been preserved from the last year of his life and his last publication, the so-called "Poésies" (really anti-poetry), suggest this. He was then twenty-four. At about the age of twenty-five, Mallarmé went through a violent crisis of a somewhat similar nature. He never gave up poetry, but his output was certainly greatly reduced as a result.

The possible causes of Valéry's crisis, the possible reasons for his renunciation of a literary career are diverse. I shall distinguish first the superficial reasons, then the probably determining ones.

One of the factors that has been mentioned, but which I would say was not a cause at all, was the impact on Valéry of his unsuccessful love for Madame "de Rov." That this produced a depression cannot be denied, but that it motivated a decision to abandon a literary career is very doubtful. About ten years later, Alain-Fournier, author of that distinguished novel, *Le Grand Meaulnes*, had a similar experience—he fell in love with a girl he passed in the street, followed her, and on one occasion talked to her briefly—and, far from having a negative effect, it proved to be a primary inspiration for his novel. And Valéry himself said (fifty years later, it is true) that in depressions caused by love affairs—he mentioned the affair of 1891–1892 and another of 1921—writing served as an "anesthetic." (See the note in a *cahier* of 1940 referred to above: *Cahiers*, vol. 23, pp. 589–590.)

A more significant factor (and I am somewhat hesitant to call it superficial) was our poet's conviction that he must earn his living and that he could not do this if he devoted himself exclusively to literature. When young Paul was sixteen, his father had died. His much older brother, Jules, then twenty-four, had

become head of the family. In 1892, Jules had not completed
his law studies: he was soon to do so and become professor
(and later dean) of the Law School at Montpellier. Paul Valéry
must have felt that he ought not to be a burden on his mother
and his brother. At that time, a really original writer (except
possibly a novelist) could hardly count on making a living from
the sales of his works. For years the books of André Gide had
pitifully small sales. But Gide was well-to-do, and this failure
hurt his pride more than his pocketbook. The difficult existence
of Alfred Jarry was to demonstrate, a few years later, what hap-
pens to an original but impecunious writer who is too unconven-
tional to succeed as a journalist and who cannot write best sellers.
Jarry's early death (at 34) was caused more by malnutrition
than by alcoholism: he was too proud to beg and too poor to
buy both food and alcohol.

I do not think, however, that the necessity of earning a living
played much part in Valéry's decision to abandon literature. The
example of Mallarmé must have showed him that a job (teach-
ing English in lycées for nearly thirty years) did not prevent a
complete dedication to poetry. That the need for Valéry to gain
employment was not terribly immediate and compelling is shown
by the fact that he did not actually get a job and earn his living
until four and one-half years later.

It is in the deeper causes that, in my opinion, we will find the
real explanation of Valéry's crisis. The title of this chapter,
"Orpheus or Narcissus?", expresses the heart of the problem in
terms of myth. In his adolescence, Valéry was faced with the
necessity of choosing between literary creation (Orpheus) and
the cultivation of his own mind (Narcissus). As a result of the
"night of Genoa," he chose the cultivation of his own mind:
remember he had said earlier, "I take delight endlessly in my
own brain." That thirty years after the night of Genoa he considered the possibility that he had made the wrong choice is
suggested in the magnificent Socratic dialogue, Eupalinos, written in 1921. Socrates discusses with his friend, Phædrus, his
hesitation at the age of eighteen. Phædrus says to him: "I can
conceive how it came about that you hesitated between building
and knowing (le construire and le connaître)." (Œuvres, II, p.
126). Socrates himself says, a little later, that "of all acts the most
complete is that of building" (Op. cit., p. 143). Regret for his

choice appears in the words: "I would have built, sung . . . what an artist I caused to perish!" (*Op. cit.*, p. 140.)[23]

Valéry's choice then, in October (or November) 1892, was to give up literature and to devote himself to cultivating his own mind. But the choice may not merely have been that he *preferred* at that moment to be Narcissus rather than Orpheus. It would seem that his now complete knowledge of Mallarmé's poetry had made his own seem quite inferior.[24] He also felt, as Mallarmé did, that poems are made with *words;* and in writing so many poems in the last few years, he may have well come to the conclusion that he had exhausted his own poetic vocabulary. He had that experience some thirty years later and made an interesting note on it in a *cahier* of February 1924. "I can't write verses any more, after five years during which I made 'many.' My verses are made with *words.* I crossed through a zone of *words* just as the earth crosses through the swarm of *Leonids* and believes in shooting stars." (*Cahiers*, vol. 9, p. 776).

I think a key to the whole question is to be found in a statement Valéry made in a letter of 1912 or 1913 to Albert Thibaudet: "Etre poète, non. Pouvoir l'être." (To be a poet, no. To be capable of being one.)[25] He was not only dissatisfied with his own poetry; he was dissatisfied with poetry in general and with literature in general. This dissatisfaction and attempts to explain it appear frequently in his published works, in his letters and in his unpublished notebooks.[26] An example is the following:

As for literature, it had often scandalized me by the degree to which it lacks rigor and logical consistency and necessity in ideas. Its objective is often minute. Our poetry is unaware of or even dreads all the epic and pathetic qualities of the intellect. . . . We do not have among us any poets who study consciousness. ("Au sujet d'*Euréka*"— *Œuvres*, I, pp. 855–856.)

The reading of Edgar Allan Poe's cosmological prose poem, *Eureka*, some months earlier,[27] had apparently served to catalyse an attitude which had surely been growing for some time. The high rating given to Poe by Baudelaire, Mallarmé, and Valéry is a constant source of surprise to American critics, who would be more inclined to accept James Russell Lowell's cruel judgment: "Three-fifths of him genius and two-fifths sheer fudge" (*A Fable for Critics*). A recent book on Poe by Patrick Quinn says: "Despite Valéry's essay on it, *Eureka* must be put aside as one of Poe's failures." [28] The "fudge" in *Eureka* is, I believe, less evident in Baudelaire's translation, which glosses over the pretentiousness and the provincialism with elegant French prose. But whether *Eureka* is as important as Valéry thought it to be is really beside the point. What is significant is Poe's effect on the young poet. He was quite explicit in one of his letters to Thibaudet: "The one who made me feel his power the most was Poe. I read in him what I needed, seized the lucid delirium that he communicates. Therefore I ceased writing verses." (Letter of 1912 or 1913, quoted in *Œuvres*, I, p. 1731.)

Thus, we see that, uncertain as to what he could accomplish as Orpheus, uncertain whether he could accomplish anything, whether *literary* accomplishment was worth anything, Valéry turned to the rôle of Narcissus.[29] We shall shortly observe in what ways he proceeded to "take delight in his own brain" during the next few years.

CHAPTER 2

The Progress of Narcissus

I *Leonardo and Monsieur Teste*

PAUL VALERY'S new orientation involved settling down definitively in Paris. In late November, 1892, he went to Paris with his mother and brother. He enjoyed the cultural life of the capital; he was a regular at Mallarmé's Tuesdays, and statements in his letters indicate that his "self-cultivation" had begun. (See *Œuvres*, I, p. 20.) Meanwhile his brother received the *agrégation de droit;* and in October, 1893, the family returned to Montpellier, where Jules became professor of law at the University.

On March 3, 1894, Paul Valéry arrived in Paris to stay. He took a room in a small hotel in the Latin Quarter, Hôtel Henri-Quatre, 12, rue Gay-Lussac, where he had stayed with his family on previous trips to Paris. He had a small room at the back, looking out over the Impasse Royer-Collard; in addition to the bed, chair, *armoire* and writing table, there was a trunk in the corner, a blackboard usually covered with equations, and on the wall a photograph of the "skeleton," a famous work by Ligier Richier, sixteenth-century French sculptor.

It was in this room that he formed the habit, continued throughout the rest of his life, whether he was at home or on his frequent travels, of getting up very early (five o'clock in the morning); and after a cup of coffee, he would light a cigarette (which he rolled himself) and spend two or three hours meditating, reasoning, calculating, and jotting down notes on these meditations, reasonings and calculations in small notebooks (the *cahiers*), of which he wrote over 250, in all, and which have been reproduced photographically in 29 quarto volumes of some 900–950 pages each.

The contents of these *cahiers* is varied; the notes range from brief jottings to organized essays, several pages in length. There are also pages of equations and formulas, and here and there a polished aphorism. In the first years, notes on mathematics and psychology dominate—an attempt to convert psychology to algebraic formulas is in evidence. Verses and rough drafts of poetry are to be found rather rarely; I know of only one case of a complete poem in the *cahiers:* an early version of "Un Feu-distinct" is found in a *cahier* of 1897 (*Cahiers,* vol. 1, p. 202). There are occasional notes on poetic theory; these become much more numerous in later volumes: 1912–1922, when Valéry had returned to the regular practice of poetry. It is also at a later period that there are frequent notes which can be called "literary criticism." These usually represent the dominating negative attitude of our poet, an attitude based upon his antipathy to literature as a profession. It is in later volumes also that we find that Valéry's mind sometimes wandered from abstract meditation; he would jot down, in very small script (suggesting that it was less important than his psychological notes?) and with often baffling abbreviations ("déjeuner avec L."), a date, and a schematic account of some event or activity.

Valéry gave titles to his early *cahiers.* The first was *Journal de bord* (logbook). He also at times used English titles, and it was, to say the least, a very personal English: *Self Book.*[1]

In addition to confiding the results of his meditations to his *cahiers,* Paul Valéry attempted to explain them in letters to his friends, André Gide and Gustave Fourment in particular, and discussed some aspects of them with his newly-formed group of Parisian associates. In two letters to Fourment of December, 1897, and January, 1898, he attempted to elucidate his theory of "arithmetica universalis" by which all human knowledge was to be unified on a mathematical basis—a theory not very successfully developed and based, at least in part, on Poe's *Eureka,* which, as we saw in the last chapter, had impressed him greatly.[2]

Paul Valéry was already beginning to acquire a reputation as a brilliant conversationalist in the circle of friends he had made in Paris: these included, in addition to André Gide and Pierre Louÿs, such men as Henri de Régnier, Marcel Schwob, Paul Léautaud, and the Franco-American, Francis Vielé-Griffin. He dazzled them with his presentation of a figure who typified for him the synthesis of artistic genius and intellectual rigor that was his ideal. This figure was Leonardo da Vinci, whom he had discovered a few years earlier. In fact the first idea of keeping notebooks may have come to him from Leonardo, whose notebooks he had come upon at the age of twenty in the Public Library of Montpellier.[3] Among those present was Léon Daudet, who, greatly impressed, suggested to Madame Juliette Adam, a literary lady of considerable importance at that moment—her recommendation was sufficient for election to the Académie Française—that she should ask Valéry to write an article on the subject for her *Nouvelle Revue*. The essay was written, not without a struggle, and appeared in the review, August 15, 1895, under the title, "Introduction à la méthode de Léonard de Vinci." Later, Valéry was to say that all his essays and similar writings were commissioned works (*des ouvrages de commande*). This was to a great extent true, but as the case just mentioned shows, the subject of the commissioned work was often a favorite theme or preoccupation of the author.

This, his first *ouvrage de commande*, was in some ways a masterpiece. Valéry was beginning to show signs of a talent which was to become remarkable later—that of adapting his prose style (his "method" he might have called it) to the subject-matter he was discussing. His earliest prose writings, such as "Sur la technique littéraire" (1889) or "Paradoxe sur l'architecte" (1891), contained a moderate, though not excessive, amount of the elaborate and obscure prose characteristic of the late symbolist period. "Introduction à la méthode de Léonard de Vinci" does not have those defects, but it must be said that the "Note et digression" (on Leonardo), written in 1919 to accompany a reprinting of the original work, is more interesting and more profitable reading. By 1919 Valéry had found his "method."

"Introduction à la méthode de Léonard de Vinci" tells us more about the young Paul Valéry than it does about the great Florentine artist and thinker. If Leonardo represented to Valéry the synthesis of artistic genius and intellectual rigor, the poet was soon to conceive a figure embodying intellectual rigor in its purest state: this was to be Monsieur Teste. Here again Poe may have provided the point of departure. As early as 1894, in one of Valéry's first *cahiers*, we find the title of a project: "Mémoires du chevalier Auguste Dupin." (*Cahiers*, vol. 1, p. 50.) Dupin was Poe's inhuman, thinking-machine detective, who first appeared in "The Murders in the rue Morgue." Teste seems to be a purified Dupin; surely he would have disdained to indulge in feats of deduction similar to those of Dupin. But if Teste is a reincarnation of Dupin, there was also in him something of the painter Edgar Degas, whom Valéry admired greatly and later came to know very well, as he related in his charming little book *Degas danse dessin* (1938). There he stated that Monsieur Teste was "to some extent *influenced* (as it is said) *by a certain Degas as I imagined him.*" (*Œuvres,* II, p. 1168.) At that moment Degas behaved as Edmond Teste would have; he refused to accept the dedication of *La Soirée avec Monsieur Teste.*[4]

When did Edmond Teste come into being? Though there is some confusion with regard to the date of composition of *La Soirée avec Monsieur Teste,*[5] evidence indicates that Valéry wrote the bulk of it and finished it during the summer of 1896,[6] while he was taking a vacation in Montpellier. It was, in one sense, another *ouvrage de commande,* written for the second— and last—issue (*circa* December, 1896) of *Le Centaure,* a handsome, deluxe review edited by several friends of Valéry's, with Valéry himself (in modest initials: "P.V."), André Gide and others, including Pierre Louÿs, listed as co-editors. Although he was later to state, "I cannot write a novel because I could never write 'The Marquise left the house at five o'clock,'"[7] *La Soirée avec Monsieur Teste* is, if too short for a novel, certainly a tale, a philosophical tale. It is the story of the acquaintance of the narrator (himself no anti-intellectual, since he begins his narrative by stating: "Stupidity is not my strong point"— *Œuvres,* II, p. 15) with a strange individual, Edmond Teste, a pure intellectual. Monsieur Teste's motto is "Que peut un homme?" (of what is a man capable?). He has "killed" the marionette in the human being; that is, he has suppressed all conventional, useless gestures and expressions, such as shaking hands, saying "good morning," etc. According to the narrator, Monsieur Teste had "succeeded in discovering laws of the mind which we do not know. Surely he must have devoted years to this study; even more surely, years more, many more years had been put into play to ripen his inventions, to turn them into his instincts. . . . He tried to find a means of giving a résumé of his work. He often said '*Maturare*' (to become mature)." (*Œuvres,* II, pp. 17–18.)

This little work (with which, as usual, Valéry was not at all

satisfied [8]) attracted no attention at first—very few people read
Le Centaure—but eventually had a considerable impact, as is
shown by the number of editions and translations (into at least
six languages). The poet continued to be preoccupied with his
intellectual superman. There are frequent notes in the *cahiers*
giving saying and opinions of Monsieur Teste. In the 1920's
Valéry published in his review, *Commerce*,[9] three more Teste
items, and a posthumous volume (1946) added five more unpublished Teste fragments. With the exception of the "Lettre
de Madame Emilie Teste" (1924), these addenda seem to me
of limited interest.[10]

II *Earning a Living*

A constant preoccupation of Valéry's earliest years in Paris was
the necessity of getting a job, of earning his living. Before leaving
Montpellier to settle in Paris, he wrote to Gide (February 26,
1894) informing him of his intentions and saying: "I must hunt
for a position that is paid, I must *establish* myself. . . . I have
a brutal need of security in all its meanings. . . . I have reached
the limits of my capacity to stand uncertainty." (Quoted in
Œuvres, II, p. 1436.) Shortly after his arrival in Paris, there was
the possibility of a job in the Armenian College in Stambul. Then,
his friend, Henri de Régnier, tried unsuccessfully to obtain for
him the position of secretary of the *Revue de Paris*. Finally, a
year later (April, 1895), following the advice of Huysmans, who
for years had made his living as a clerk in a government office,
he entered the competition for a job in the War Office. Although
he was under the suspicion of being a sort of a symbolist poet
(like "Varlaine"—*sic*), he was in June declared qualified.
(*Œuvres*, I, p. 22.) But he had to wait for nearly two years
(May 5, 1897) before he was actually appointed.

In the meantime he had made two trips to London; the first
in June, 1894, was a visit to his aunt De Rin. On his return he
wrote to Gide (July 14, 1894): "the remarkable nullity of English
literature surprised and charmed me." (Quoted in *Œuvres*, II,
p. 1438.) His second trip was in the spring of 1896. Whether he
had nothing more in view than a temporary job (translating
articles on South Africa for the "Chartered Company") or
whether he was aiming at something more permanent, I do not
know. At any rate he did not stay long. He had left for England

March 30; by May 18 he was back in Paris. (*Œuvres*, I, p. 23.)
But while he was in England, William Ernest Henley, editor of
the *New Review*, and also a poet, asked Valéry to write an article
on the threat of the aggressively developing Germany. This
article appeared (in French) in the review, January, 1897, with
the title, "La Conquête allemande." When the first World War
broke out, the article was remembered, reprinted (in the *Mercure
de France*, 1er septembre 1915), and found to be strangely
prophetic.

As Paul Valéry was to reveal much later ("Avant-Propos" of
Regards sur le monde actuel, 1931—*Œuvres,* II, pp. 913 ff.), it
was at about this time that he began to develop the prejudice
against history that was to be one of his most celebrated and
most controversial theories. In the late nineties

> I thought I had to study history and even master it thoroughly to have
> an exact idea of the present day. I knew that all the heads concerned
> with the future of nations were nourished on it. But, as for me, I found
> only a *horrible mixture.* Under the name of the History of Europe, I
> saw only a collection of parallel chronicles which were intermingled in
> spots. No method seemed to have preceded the choice of the "facts,"
> decided their importance, determined clearly the object pursued. I
> noticed an unbelievable number of implicit hypotheses and ill-defined
> entities. (*Op. cit.,* p. 915).

He continued meditating along these lines, and he discussed his
opinion in letters as early as 1906,[11] but did not express these
theories publicly until the late twenties: "Notes sur la grandeur
et la décadence de l'Europe," 1927; "De l'histoire," 1931; "Discours de l'histoire," 1932.

I believe that it was during this short stay in London that
there took place a curious episode mentioned in a *cahier* of
January, 1925:

> One day in London I wanted to hang myself. The day was yellow and
> sulphury. Wreaths of smoke dripped down from the roofs into the
> street, where they rolled around. A Sunday. . . .
> While I was looking for a rope in the closet, I found a volume of
> Aurélien Scholl.[12] I laughed and I was *saved.* (*Cahiers,* vol. 10,
> p. 442.)

In the course of my discussion of the progress of Valéry-Narcissus, it has been apparent that Valéry-Orpheus, the creator, was not dead. The conception and presentation of such a Narcissus-like character as Monsieur Teste was itself a notable act of creation. And I propose now to examine the poetry of Valéry's majority and to show that, while the production of Valéry-Orpheus, the singer, had diminished greatly in quantity, it had augmented notably in quality. In the period between his abandonment of literature in 1892 and his marriage in 1900, Paul Valéry wrote at least five or six poems, four of which were published at the time: "Eté" and "Vue" in the first number of *Le Centaure* (spring 1896), "Valvins," written for a manuscript album presented to Mallarmé in the spring of 1897, containing poems of homage by twenty poets, and published in *La Coupe* (February, 1898), and "Anne" in *La Plume* of December 1, 1900.[13] In addition to these I must mention "Un Feu distinct," which was not to be published until the *Album de vers anciens* of 1920, but which, as I said above, is found in rough draft, considerably different from the final version, in a *cahier* of 1897. (*Cahiers*, vol. 1, p. 202.)[14] One other poem, "Profusion du soir, poème abandonné," which was not to be published until the *Quelques vers* of 1926, according to a note in volume "C" of the *Œuvres complètes* (published in 1933), was written in 1899.

All of these are poems of real distinction; "Eté" and "Vue" seem to me particularly fine. The images characterizing summer in "Eté" are dazzling: "Eté, roche d'air pur, et toi, ardente ruche, / O mer! . . ." (Summer, rock of pure air, and, thou, ardent hive, / O sea! . . .) "Et toi, maison brûlante, Espace, cher Espace / Tranquille, où l'arbre fume et perd quelques oiseaux . . ." (And thou, burning house, Space, dear Space / Tranquil, where the tree smokes and loses a few birds . . .)

I cite "Vue" in entirety: this short poem, in verses of seven syllables, with the rime scheme of what is called in English a "Shakespearian" sonnet, but in French a *quatorzain,* shows Valéry as a disciple of Mallarmé, but a very original one, and also shows that at the age of twenty-five he had reached a degree of hermeticism that he was not to exceed twenty-one years later with *La Jeune Parque.*

VUE

Si la plage penche, si
L'ombre sur l'œil s'use et pleure
Si l'azur est larme, ainsi
Au sel des dents pures s'affleure

La vierge fumée ou l'air
Que berce en soi puis expire
Vers l'eau debout d'une mer
Assoupie en son empire

Celle qui sans les ouïr
Si la lèvre au vent remue
Se joue à évanouir
Mille mots vains où se mue

Sous l'humide éclair des dents
Le très doux feu du dedans.
(*Œuvres*, I, p. 84.
©*Editions Gallimard.*)

(VUE. If the beach leans, if / The shadow on the eye is worn and weeps / If the azure is a tear, so / On the salt of the pure teeth is leveled / The virgin smoke or the air / Which is cradled in self then expires / Toward the upstanding water of the sea / Becalmed in its empire / By the one who without hearing them / If the lip trembles in the wind / Plays at causing to vanish / A thousand idle words in which is transfigured / Under the damp flash of the teeth / The most gentle interior fire.)

As I stated above, Valéry took up his job in the War Ministry in May, 1897. Although he was serious about this new undertaking and endeavored to interest himself in it, he complained of the difficulty he had in adapting himself to the drudgery of office work.[15]

I should like to be able to say that the stand Valéry took on the great affair of the moment, the Dreyfus Case (he was an "anti-Dreyfusard"), was purely a matter of expediency, but I cannot. With the Army almost solidly endeavoring to establish for all time that Dreyfus was guilty, it would have been most unwise for a modest *employé* of the War Ministry to take another attitude. But Valéry seems to have been a convinced "anti-Dreyfusard." When the forgeries of Colonel Henry were revealed (summer of 1898), when it became known that the "proofs" of Dreyfus's guilt were fakes, and when Henry killed himself, Emile Drumont's paper, *La Libre parole*, organ of anti-semitism and the lunatic fringe of the extreme right, opened a subscription to aid Henry's widow and published long lists of subscribers and the amounts subscribed. Many of the names were accompanied by disgusting anti-semitic slogans. On one of the lists we read "P. Valéry . . . 1 fr." This *could* be interpreted as a token manifestation. But Valéry intended more than a token, as is shown clearly by the following statement, in a letter to Gustave Fourment (March 9, 1900):

Yesterday I received from Kolbassine a registered letter—full of insults. I had had no news of him for two years. He saw my name, with my little statement, in the recently published lists of subscribers for Madame Henry. . . . I replied to him in three lines, calm and decent but energetic.[16]

This letter would make it seem that the subscription list which I found in *La Libre parole* is not the same one as that to which Valéry referred. Paul Léautaud, in his *Journal littéraire*, tells of accompanying Valéry when he went to subscribe to "the Henry monument." Valéry gave five francs and Léautaud two. Valéry's statement was "not without reflexion." [17]

It is hard to believe that the skeptically minded and generally misanthropic Valéry could have accepted the thesis that Colonel Henry was a self-sacrificing hero: he was alleged (by Charles Maurras, for instance) to have made these forgeries because the "real" proofs of Dreyfus's guilt, if published, would have precipitated a war with Germany! There is evidence[18] to show that Valéry was annoyed at the propaganda of his liberal friends (one, Fénéon, was an anarchist), and personally, at least at that moment, decidedly hostile to democracy. His preoccupation with the intellectual superman had led him to a great interest in the man wielding extreme power, the dictator, the tyrant. Examples of this are the sonnet "César" (*Œuvres*, I, pp. 79–80), probably written in the 90's, and the references in the *cahiers* to the Emperor Tiberius,[19] to Napoleon, and to Caesar. A *cahier* written late in 1898 contains the following multilingual slogans: "Le César de soi-même / El Cesar de su mismo / Il Cesare di se stesso / The Cesar (sic) of himself." (*Cahiers*, vol. 1, p. 274.)

The death of Stéphane Mallarmé, September 9, 1898, was a great shock to Paul Valéry and, in a sense, a turning point in his life, since his marriage, two years later, was, as he felt, a way of carrying out the wishes of the older poet. The death of Mallarmé meant the end of his little pension as a retired lycée professor, and his wife and daughter were thus destitute, at least for the time being: a few years later the poet's daughter married Doctor Edmond Bonniot. A number of letters in the Gide-Valéry correspondence reveal that Valéry, Gide, and Vielé-Griffin found discreet and tactful ways of coming to the aid of the Mallarmé ladies. It was during one of this visits to Madame Mallarmé and her daughter at Valvins, the village on the Seine where Mallarmé spent his summers for many years, that Paul Valéry met some young friends of Geneviève Mallarmé—Julie Manet, daughter of Eugène Manet (brother of Edouard Manet) and the painter Berthe Morisot, and her cousins, Paule and Jeannie Gobillard.

Up to then, with the possible exception of the "affair" with the mysterious Madame "de Rov." in Montpellier, Valéry's sentimental and/or sex life seems to have been casual and unimportant. At least such is the impression given by a curious list found in a *cahier* of 1899. It is headed "Exercices particuliers" (Special exercises):

Potential	Rov.
Semi	Pin (his cousin, Pinetta Rin?)
" "	M. T. V.
Complete	Bath.
	Clau.
	Loul.
	Loulboul
Various	H. Fin-Hill
	Fan.
	Jon. . .
	Zo+
	Carraci
	Me

Below this is written: "All this is in no way extraordinary."
(*Cahiers,* vol. 1, p. 733.) The names (not very legible) listed
above have not been identified, except for "Rov.", the lady of
Montpellier, and "Bath." Other biographers of Valéry have said
that in 1895 he had a mistress named Bathilde, who was an
equestrienne in the Circus.[20] The "Loul" may well be the "Lou-
lou" of whom Valéry earlier had given a brief portrait (a *cahier*
of 1898, vol. 1, p. 503), calling her a "délicieuse catin" (delightful
strumpet).

In February, 1900, Paul Valéry and Jeannie Gobillard became
engaged; they were married May 31 of the same year. On June
8, the young husband wrote to his friend André Gide: "Sono
felicissimo" (I am most happy).[21]

The young couple lived for two years, along with Jeannie's
sister, Paule (a painter of some talent), in an apartment on the
Avenue Victor-Hugo. Then, in July 1902, they moved to the
apartment 40, rue de Villejust (now rue Paul-Valéry), in which
they were to live until Paul Valéry's death, and where Madame
Valéry still lives.

As a conclusion to my account of Paul Valéry's life and activities as a bachelor in Paris, I reproduce (on the next page) this
curious autobiographical sketch or schema that is found in a
cahier of 1899:

Not all of this is legible, and there are a few of the legible
notations that I am unable to explain. The left-hand column lists
Valéry's mental preoccupations at the dates indicated in the
second column. First "Romanticism," then, in 1888–1889, "Orne-
ment," then 1889–1890, "Poetry" and "Stéphane Mallarmé." I
cannot figure out exactly what he means by "Combinations" in
1890–1891, or by "N + s" in 1891–1892. At that point a horizontal
line, with "Réforme" written at the right, indicates the great
crisis of October, 1892. Then come "D"(?) "Symmetry" in 1892,
"Mathematics" in 1893 and "Psychology" 1894 to 1899. The notes
in the *cahiers* for this period bear out the fact that psychology
was then a major preoccupation of Valéry.

The third column gives the superficial facts of his career:
Philosophy at the Lycée in 1887, Droit (law) at the University,
1888 and 1889, interrupted 1889–1890 by Military Service, and
resumed in 1890–1891. I cannot guess the meaning of "St" at
the date 1896.

The last column lists, not always legibly, events and people. 1887: the death of his father; 1889–1890: friendship with Pierre Louÿs and André Gide; 1890–1891: (and following) his unrequited love for Madame de Rov.; 1891–1892; after the "Réforme" in 1892 what I read as "Mars Paris (Londres)"—which is puzzling, since he went to Paris in November 1892, and did not go to London until 1894; 1894: "C" (?); 1895: "Vinci, manœuvres" (28 days of Army training?); "Bath." November 1895 (this is the circus equestrienne referred to above). An interest in Napoleon is indicated, as is his trip to London in 1896, his article on Germany, the death of Mallarmé. "Teste August" and what, in view of its position on the page, should be "96" but looks more like "95."

The first decade of the twentieth century was, in Valéry's work, the period of the least activity. No new work of his was published then except for "L'Amateur de poèmes," a prose poem written for Walch's *Anthologie des poètes français contemporains* (1906) and an essay, "Etudes," written at the request of Gide for his new periodical, *la Nouvelle Revue française,* where it appeared December 1, 1909. The *cahiers* suggest that Valéry's intellectual life was much less active than before or after. Between 1900 and 1913 the *cahiers* are contained in three volumes (volumes 2, 3, and 4) with a total of 2,762 pages. By contrast, in the thirteen years following, the *cahiers* fill seven volumes (volumes 5, 6, 7, 8, 9, 10, and 11), with a total of 6,432 pages. One can assume that it was adjustment to family life, a son in 1903 and a daughter in 1906, and to a new job, that caused this. In the summer of 1900, not long after his marriage, Valéry obtained a six-month leave from the War Ministry for what he thought was a temporary position as private secretary to Edouard Lebey, director of the French press service, the Agence Havas. He kept the job until Lebey's death, in February 1922.

In an article in *L'Arche,* October, 1945, André Gide summarized as follows Valéry's duties and his relation to his employer:

It was a confidential position, where Valéry had every opportunity to make use of his sagacity and his competence in political, diplomatic and financial matters, the soundness of his judgments, his probity, his tact and finally the exquisite courtesy of his manner and the delicacy of his feelings. He would speak of the old man, to whom he had become devoted, with great deference. M. Lebey was afflicted with Parkinson's disease, because of which he could not control his movements. To those who came to see him he would say, since he couldn't hold out his hand which his infirmity caused to shake: "Stop my hand, please." Seated in a big armchair, he listened to the reading of the newspapers and of the sermons of Bourdaloue (which he preferred to Bossuet's); but Valéry admitted to me that he often skipped pages. That lasted months, years. And surely Valéry learned a lot from that wise old man, in those delicate operations which tested the practical qualities of his mind.[22]

Since my principal concern is Valéry the writer and the thinker, and not Valéry the good husband and father and the tactful private secretary of Edouard Lebey, I shall give no further details for the period 1900–1912. For this I refer the reader to the frequently mentioned *Introduction biographique* (*Œuvres*, I, pp. 26–35). I close this chapter, entitled "The Progress of Narcissus," with the remark that marriage and a happy family life are a surprising development in the career of a Narcissus.

CHAPTER 3

The Return of Orpheus

I *Reluctant Poet*

A JUSTIFICATION of the title of this chapter is the fact that, as far as I know, Paul Valéry's return to poetry was marked by the publication of a sonnet entitled "Orphée," in the review *Les Fêtes* of September 15, 1913. Since this publication has been completely forgotten, I shall give all the information about it that I have been able to discover.

I know of the present existence of only one number of this obscure review, *Les Fêtes*. The Bibliothèque littéraire Jacques Doucet contains a copy of the January 15, 1914 issue: "*Les Fêtes*, revue mensuelle, chez Eugène Figuière et Cie, Tome IV, no. 39." This issue published a sonnet by Valéry entitled "Fée": it is an "intermediate" version of the sonnet "Féerie" of the *Album de vers anciens*, of which the original version, entitled "Blanc," had appeared in *L'Ermitage* of December, 1890.[1] Proceeding on the assumption that other poems of Valéry might well have been published in the same review, I hunted for it, not only in the public libraries of Paris, but on the quays and in the second-hand book shops. The second-hand book dealers were not interested—the commercial value of this old magazine being nonexistent—and my search was vain. But I did discover, at the Bibliothèque Nationale, three volumes (1910–1913) of *Annales des Fêtes et cérémonies civiles*, a review which was the predecessor of *Les Fêtes*. The last number of the *Annales des Fêtes* (August, 1913) has bound with it an announcement of its successor and also what I take to be a facsimile (or the original?) of the cover page of the number of September 15, 1913, including the "Sommaire," which lists "Paul Valéry. . . . Orphée. . . . 22." I consider this sufficient proof that Valéry's sonnet "Orphée" was published on the date mentioned. It is a reasonable assumption, which I hope someday to verify, that the text is an intermediate form, differing from the text published in *La*

Conque in May 1891 (*Œuvres,* I, pp. 1539-1540) and from the final version, published in the *Quelques vers* of 1926, and from then on as part of the *Album de vers anciens* (*Œuvres,* I, pp. 76-77).[2]

I stated confidently that the "Orphée" published in *Les Fêtes* was different from the earlier version, because it is known that the first step in Paul Valéry's return to poetry was the revision of his early poems, that is, those that he considered worth republishing. Much later the poet described his return to poetry in two articles: "Le Prince et la Jeune Parque" (first published as "Comment je revins à la poésie" in *Les Annales,* April, 1927) and "Fragments des mémoires d'un poème," published in the *Revue de Paris,* December 15, 1937. But already, in 1915, in two letters to his old friend, Albert Coste (published in 1946 in *Paul Valéry vivant,* and reprinted in *Lettres à quelques-uns,* 1952, and, in part, in the *Œuvres,* II, pp. 1576-1480), he had given another, and as I shall show farther on, a rather odd version of his return to poetry. The most direct account of this turning point in Valéry's life is found in his correspondence with Gide.

The first mention of a project of publication of Valéry's earlier writings is these lines in a letter from Gide, May 31, 1912: "You will take it upon yourself, will you not, to send to Gaston Gallimard, 79, rue Saint-Lazare, your poems, La Soirée avec Teste, la Méthode de Léonard, the different fragments from that period, in short, everything that is to go into this first volume of your works." [3] Gide himself possessed a manuscript of Valéry's poetry,[4] but as he says in the same letter, he had put it away so "avariciously" (*sic—avarement*) that in the rush of his departure for Cuverville he was unable to find it.

Gide had founded the periodical, *la Nouvelle Revue française* in 1909, with Gaston Gallimard as publisher, and two years later he and Gallimard decided to extend their activities to publishing books. So, early in 1912, he went with the publisher to see Valéry and put before him the project of issuing as a book his early writings, both poetry and prose. As the following quotations show, Valéry was not easily convinced of the desirability of this project.

On June 5 Gide wrote to Valéry: "I am sorry I couldn't be there (in Paris) to talk to you about your book; but this first volume, completely a retrospective, doesn't seem to me to cause any difficulties. I am at your disposal, however, if there is any catch." (*Op. cit.*, p. 424.) Over a month later (July 19), he wrote—he was back in Cuverville after a short trip to Paris during which he was unable to see Valéry—"I would have liked to push you a bit on this book, and get you to make the right decision. Gallimard is afraid to annoy you by asking insistently for your texts." (*Op. cit.*, pp. 424–425.) Valéry answered (July 21): "As for the book . . . my hesitation exists. A very simple mixture of lack of interest, of pride, of fatigue in even thinking of galley proofs, of that scorn, innate in myself, for my fundamental state of non-completion. . . ." (*Op. cit.*, p. 427.) He went on to indicate that he was, nevertheless, concerned about *tomorrow*, which meant: what would he do for a living after the death of Edouard Lebey, an old man in frail health? "If I didn't absolutely, with the very first words, refuse to get into print, it was exactly because I was thinking of that *tomorrow*. I can *tomorrow* find myself in a very embarrassing situation, and I say to myself that, in spite of everything, perhaps if a book had been published, that would help." (*Op. cit.*, p. 428.) Four days later he wrote again to Gide: "Gallimard came to see me Tuesday. I think, alas, that that's it." (*Op. cit.*, p. 429.) Which means that they had reached an agreement. Gallimard had had a typescript prepared (apparently copied from the reviews in which the poems and prose had appeared) which was given to Valéry for correction and approval. (*Op. cit.*, p. 423, n. 4.)

A number of letters in the following months discuss various publishing possibilities; should there be a mixture of prose and verse, entitled *Mélanges?* Should the verse be published separately in a deluxe *plaquette?* Actually, no decision was made, and, in the meantime—exactly when we don't know, but surely before the end of 1912[5]—Valéry had (1) started to revise his early poems, and (2) begun to write a poem of some length, which was to become *La Jeune Parque.*

What made him decide to revise his early poems is well indicated in a passage in "Fragments de mémoires d'un poème," where he speaks of his state of mind:

Those who had asked me to publish my old verses had collected and copied these scattered little poems and had given me the collection.

. . . One day of fatigue and boredom, chance (which accomplishes everything) brought it about that this copy came to the surface of the disorder of my papers. I was in a somber mood. Never did poems fall under the scrutiny of colder glances. They found in their author a man who had become completely rebellious to their effects. This hostile father leafed through the thin booklet of his complete poetry in which he found nothing but reasons for being glad he had given up the game. If he stopped at a certain page, considering the weakness of most of the verses, he felt a strong desire to strengthen them, to melt down the musical substance. . . . Here and there were rather graceful verses, which merely accused the others and spoiled the general effect, for unevenness in a work seemed to me then the worst evil. . . .

I soon found it amusing to try to correct a few verses, without attaching a shadow of a purpose to the little local pleasure which is procured by a free and light bit of work. . . . (*Œuvres*, I, p. 1480.)

The revision of the early poems seems to have been well under way in the summer of 1913. In a letter to his wife of July, 1913, from Perros-Guirec on the coast of Brittany, he complained that he was making no headway with his new poem (*La Jeune Parque*): "The poem isn't moving. It is stuck in the sand. Useless to go over it. Nothing works. . . ." But the seashore, the ripples of the waves on the sand and on the pebbles helped with the revision of an older poem; he said that they suggested the verse "Creuse, creuse, rumeur de soif" (dig, dig, rumor of thirst). (*Œuvres*, I, pp. 36–37.) This is an intermediate state of the tenth verse of the sonnet, "Naissance de Vénus." In the text published in *L'Ermitage* in June, 1891, this verse was "Croulent sous ses pieds fins et la grève facile" (crumble under her delicate feet and the easy strand), while the final form is "Croule, creuse rumeur de soif, et le facile" (crumbles, hollow rumor of thirst and the easy). (*Œuvres*, I, pp. 77, 1541–1543.)

Before continuing an examination of Valéry's revision of his early poems, which I have touched upon here only incidentally, in an effort to fix the date when he was engaged in the process of revision, I shall have further information to furnish on the various reasons or justifications, some bizarre, which Valéry gave for his return to poetry.

It would seem that Paul Valéry felt that his return to writing poetry was the betrayal of an ideal—the ideal of Monsieur Teste, for instance—and that he had to find excuses to justify himself.

One of these excuses, expressed in a letter to Gide which I quoted above, was his concern for the precariousness of his financial situation. This concern, which some biographers have called unjustified, or, at least, exaggerated, was a constant one. The publication of books *might* be advantageous, financially. As it turned out (I shall explain this later) it was!

Another type of excuse was expressed in a letter of 1915 to Albert Coste and one of 1916 to André Breton. It was wartime, and there was a curious neurosis in all of Europe in those years, a neurosis that reached America in 1917. According to this neurosis, the War was something sacred and had to be the complete and never-ceasing obsession of all patriots. It was as if Valéry felt obliged to answer the question: "What! You write *poetry* during the *War?*" (Instead of chauvinistic and what now seems ridiculous propaganda, like Maurice Barrès.)

Valéry's letter to Coste, with whom he had been out of touch for a long time, is a brief autobiography: "Now it's War. It will last long enough perhaps for me to be called up.[6] I suffered at first from doing nothing. The times were too tense to continue long-lasting exercises; do you know what I am doing now? I am repairing, repainting and varnishing old poems. It is minute and ridiculous, but it is traditional: at each terrible epoch of humanity you have always seen a man sitting in a corner, polishing his style and stringing beads." (*L.à q.,* pp. 103–104.)

His letter to Breton, about a year later, was similar, but more apologetic. (The young Breton, not yet twenty, even then made already such an imposing impression upon people that they felt obliged to justify to him their way of existence.)

I am writing verses, imposed task and artifice, a game forgotten long ago. Why? There are reasons. If nothing else, the state of war, too exciting to admit, in addition, rigorous analyses carried out thoroughly (other reasons, too!). It is an old-fashioned type of poetry and I am prolonging it indefinitely.[7] Nothing that you or I like. I figure it is the kind of work done by Latin versifiers. There were formerly rhetoricians, during the times of Attila and Genseric, who masticated hexameters in a corner. For whom? For what? [8] (*Œuvres,* II, p. 1615.)

Some years later Valéry summed up the conditions of his return to poetry more objectively and less defensively:

La Nouvelle Revue française, whose publishing house had just been
founded, asked me about 1913 to collect my old poems. I refused for
a long time. Gide and Gallimard were persistant. They prepared
typed copies of various little poems lying in reviews of yesterday, and
I found myself in the presence of my old poems which I contemplated
with an eye bereft of illusion and devoid of tolerance. I took pleasure
in altering them with all the freedom and all the detachment of a man
who for a long period had been unaccustomed to bother with poetry.
I formed anew a certain taste for this sort of work, of which I had
lost the habit, and I got the idea of writing one last piece, a sort of
farewell to those games of adolescence. . . . That was the origin of
La Jeune Parque.[9]

It is to be hoped that some day a complete study will be made
of the process of revision that turned the poems published in
La Conque, La Syrinx, L'Ermitage, etc., 1890–1892, into the
poems of the *Album de vers anciens.*[10] This is neither the place
nor the time. Jean Hytier, in the notes of the *Œuvres,* gave all
the variants of the printed texts and those of the few manuscripts
that were at his disposal. These provide materials for a study of
the revisions of the early poems, but the study would not be
complete. It is known that a considerable number of autograph
original manuscripts and rough drafts are in existence, and it is
possible that these will some day be available to scholars. J. R.
Lawler's study of "Orphée" (previously referred to) gave an
example of what can be done in comparing two different states
of a poem (and I attempted something similar with the four
"Féeries" in my "Nuit magique de Paul Valéry," *Revue d'Histoire
littéraire de la France,* vol. 60, pp. 199–212, avril-juin, 1960).

Here I shall summarize briefly the extent and nature of Valéry's revisions in the years 1912 and following. They were considerable, sometimes changing a poem completely, and, I feel,
always creative; that is, they constitute an improvement. Of the
twenty-one poems in the editions of the *Album de vers anciens*
that can be considered definitive (from 1931 on), eleven had
been first printed in the years 1890–1892. Two of these, "La
Fileuse" and "Hélène," had been revised extensively as early as
1900 (for their publication in Van Bever and Léautaud's *Poètes
d'aujourd'hui*) and little changed thereafter. "Orphée," "Naissance de Vénus," "Féerie, "Baignée," "Au Bois dormant," and
"Narcisse parle" received extensive modifications before being

reprinted in 1920, and evidence that I have already presented shows that at least three of these were revised between 1912 and 1914.

An example of the type of revision done by Valéry in 1912–1914 is the case of the poem which, originally entitled "Blanc," became "Fée" in 1914, then got its final title, "Féerie" in 1920 (with a variant of the same poem, "Même Féerie," first appearing in 1926). We have here one definite example of revisions made between 1912 and 1914. I shall give here the 1890 and 1914 versions (with translations), and then a few comments on the revisions.

BLANC

La lune mince verse une lueur sacrée,
Comme une jupe d'un tissu d'argent léger
Sur les degrés d'argent où va l'enfant songer,
Chair de perle que moule une gaze nacrée.

Sur les cygnes dolents qui frôlent les roseaux,
—Galères blanches et carènes lumineuses—
Elle effeuille des lys et des roses neigeuses
Et les pétales font des cercles sur les eaux.

Puis—pensive—la fille aux chimères subtiles
Voit se tordre les flots comme de blancs reptiles
A ses pieds fins chaussés d'hermine et de cristal;

La mer confuse des fleurs pudiques l'encense
Car elle enchante de sa voix, frêle métal,
La Nuit lactée et douce et le pâle silence.
(*Œuvres*, I, p. 1543. © *Editions Gallimard*)

(WHITE. The thin moon pours a sacred light, / Like a skirt of a fabric of light silver / On the ivory steps where the Child dreams, / Pearly flesh molded by a nacreous gauze. / On the melancholy swans who brush through the reeds, / —White galleys and luminous keels— / She strips off the flowers of lilies and roses / And the petals make circles on the waters. / Then—pensive—the girl of subtle whims / Sees the waves twisting like white reptiles / At her delicate feet shod with ermine and crystal. / The confused sea of modest flowers worships her, / For she

enchants with her voice, frail metal, / The milky and gentle night
and the pale silence.)

FÉE

La lune mince verse une lueur sacrée
Toute une jupe d'un tissu d'argent léger
Sur les bases de marbre où va l'Ombre songer
Que suit d'un char de perle une gaze nacrée.

Pour les cygnes soyeux qui frôlent les roseaux
De carènes de plume à demi-lumineuse,
Elle effeuille infinie une rose neigeuse
Et les pétales font des cercles sur les eaux.

Mouvant l'Ombre l'iris de présences subtiles
Son frisson sur les flots coule de blancs reptiles
A ses pieds fins glacés d'hermine et de cristal;

La chair confuse des molles roses commence
A frémir, si d'un chant le diamant fatal
Fèle toute la nuit d'un fil de fée immense.
(*Œuvres*, I, 1543–1544.
© *Editions Gallimard*.)

(FAY. The thin moon pours a sacred light / A full skirt of a
fabric of light silver / On the marble bases where the Shadow
goes to dream / Where a nacreous gauze follows a pearly char-
iot. / For the silky swans which brush through the reeds / With
feathery keels half-luminous, / She infinitely strips off the flowers
from a snowy rose / And the petals make circles on the waters. /
Moving the Shadow the rainbow of subtle presences / Her shud-
der flows white reptiles on the waves / At her delicate feet
glacéed with ermine and crystal. / The confused flesh of the soft
roses begins / To tremble if the fatal diamond of a song / Splits
the whole night with an immense, fairylike shaft.)

The small change in the second verse is not very important—
possibly an improvement harmonically. In the third verse, however, there is a definite change: the "Enfant," a person at least,
becomes an "Ombre." The changes in the second quatrain are
few in number but significant. The adjective "dolents" of verse 5,
so characteristically 1890, is replaced by "soyeux," and the image
of verse 7 is simplified and strengthened. The massive "galères"

of verse 6, out of keeping with the picture, also disappear. Then the very explicit syntactical organization of the first tercet is scrapped, and replaced by vagueness, which continues in the second tercet. But the vagueness does not become incomprehensibility. We do not know too well who or what is the "Ombre" which replaces the "Enfant," but in both cases the action, if that is what it can be called, is similar. In the first and second verses of the last tercet, the imagery becomes richer, as for example, the voice, characterized in "Blanc" as "frêle métal," a good choice for sound but less successful for sense, becomes in "Fée" "d'un chant le diamant fatal." The final verse in "Fée" seems to me a doubtful improvement over "Blanc."

This leads me to point out that, as I have just demonstrated, Valéry showed progress in the 1912–1914 revisions of his poems, but the process was continued in the years following, and the "Féerie," published in 1920, incorporating revisions of an uncertain date between 1914 and 1920, is a further improvement. Almost all the revisions are in the tercets. At the risk of being accused of getting far ahead of my present stage in Valéry's life, I present "Féerie," with a few comments:

FÉERIE

La lune mince verse une lueur sacrée,
Toute une jupe d'un tissu d'argent léger,
Sur les bases de marbre où vient l'Ombre songer
Que suit d'un char de perle une gaze nacrée.

Pour les cygnes soyeux qui frôlent les roseaux
De carènes de plume à demi lumineuse
Elle effeuille infinie une rose neigeuse
Dont les pétales font des cercles sur les eaux . . .

Est-ce vivre? . . . O désert de volupté pâmée
Où meurt le battement faible de l'eau lamée,
Usant le seuil secret des échos de cristal . . .

La chair confuse des molles roses commence
A frémir, si d'un cri le diamant fatal
Fêle d'un fil de jour toute la fable immense.
                    (*Œuvres*, I, pp. 77–78.
                         © *Editions Gallimard.*)

(ENCHANTMENT. The only changes in the quatrains are, line
3 "vient" (comes) for "va", and, line 8 "dont" (whose) for "Et
les." TERCETS: Is this living? . . . O desert of rapturous pleasure / Where dies away the feeble beating of the laminated water,
/ Wearing away the threshold of the echoes of crystal . . . / The
confused flesh of the soft roses begins / To tremble, if the fatal
diamond of a cry / Splits with a shaft of daylight all the immense
fable.)

The changes in the quatrains are minor improvements. The
big revision is in the first tercet, which is completely new and far
superior. In the 1914 version, although the "Enfant" of "Blanc"
had become an "Ombre," she still had feet, shod (the word
"glacés" which replaced "chaussés" is almost untranslateable)
with ermine and crystal—a possible reminiscence of *Cendrillon*.
The transformation of a *fin-de-siècle* fairytale into an impression
of dazzling enchantment takes place with the complete revision
of this tercet. The changes in the second tercet are small in number but significant. "Cri" instead of "chant" goes better with both
the sound and the sense of "diamant" and "fil," and the awkward
"fil de fée immense" (what is a "fil de fée" and how could it be
"immense"?) is happily rearranged.

II *Something Like the Recitative of Glück*

La Jeune Parque, written between 1912 and 1917, the first completely new poem of Valéry after his return to poetry, is his long-
est (512 verses), and, as is agreed upon by all, including Valéry
himself, his most obscure poem. It has been studied and expli-
cated by many, the most complete of the studies being the handsome critical edition published in the series of the Club du Meilleur Livre.[11] Valéry himself explained not only the genesis of the
poem and his intentions in writing it, but attempted to justify its
obscurity—primarily, according to the author himself, a result
of the difficult subject—all this in the articles I referred to above.

Not one of these exegeses or explications, interesting and in-
genious as they may be, has succeeded, for this reader at least,
in clarifying *La Jeune Parque,* which for him remains a conglo-
meration of harmonious, often suavely beautiful, but cloudy fragments in which an occasional spark of meaning shines through.
Nevertheless, I feel that it will be useful to place before the

reader, my own reader, the general reader rather than the specialist, (1) Valéry's own explanation of the genesis of the poem and his intentions in writing it, (2) his interpretation of the subject-matter, and (3) a summary of a representative (and excellent) exegesis of the poem.

Valéry discussed the genesis of *La Jeune Parque* on a number of occasions: in the two published essays previously referred to —"Le Prince et la Jeune Parque" (1927—*Œuvres,* I, pp. 1491–1496) and "Fragments des mémoires d'un poème" (1937—*Œuvres,* I, pp. 1464–1491),—also in several letters to friends, letters which have been published and the most significant parts of which were reprinted in the *Œuvres* (I, pp. 1614–1628), and also, very briefly, in the note, "Comme j'ai fait la J. P.," in a *cahier* of 1917. In all of these accounts the author insists that the point of departure was a preoccupation with *form,* and the temptation to write something that would be a *modulation,* something like the recitatives in an opera by Glück. In "Fragments des mémoires d'un poème" he states: *"La Jeune Parque* was a quest, literally indefinite, into what could be attempted in poetry that would be analogous to what is called 'modulation' in music. . . . This production, which evolved, in a sense, from the 'form' towards the 'content' . . ." (*Œuvres,* I, pp. 1473–1474.) In "Le Prince et le Jeune Parque" he is more specific:

I caught myself in the act of versifying. I recognized in myself the concerns and the worries of a poet. . . ." (*Œuvres,* I, p. 1492.) (But as he returned to poetry, he discovered) that after the felicities of planning and the promises of beautiful things which are glimpsed, after one has been beguiled by these divine murmurs of the interior voice and after pure fragments have come out from what does not exist, you must finally get down to the labor, articulate these sounds, write these fragments, question your whole intellect, journey through your whole mind—and—wait. . . .

I plunged into this labor. My scheme was to compose a sort of discourse of which the succession of verses would be developed or deduced in such a way that the work as a whole would give an impression analogous to that of the recitatives of the past. Those found in Glück, especially in the *Alceste,* had given me much subject for meditation. I envied that moving line.

Soon I came up against eternal difficulties. Having spent almost a

whole day in making, unmaking and remaking some part of my poem,
I got that sort of desperate disgust with it that all artists know.
(*Œuvres*, I, pp. 1492–1493.)

This same essay goes on to point out that he was given the
inspiration (or confidence) to go on by a *feuilleton* of Adolphe
Brisson (*Le Temps*, December 1, 1913)[12] in which the critic
analyzes and quotes extensively from Prince George of Hohen-
zollern's detailed and curiously revealing notes on the diction of
the great early nineteenth-century actress, Rachel. How and why
this constituted the necessary catalyzing agent is not made very
clear: I don't believe Valéry was very certain about it himself.[13]

The note "Comme j'ai fait la J. P." in the *cahier* of June, 1917,
has a few details suggesting that the influence of the alexandrines
of Racine was also significant at that period. He cites a portion
of a famous verse from *Phèdre:* "le jour n'est pas plus pur que—"
and in abbreviated form refers to a passage from *Esther* ("Pri.
d'Esther"—Esther's prayer) and one from *Athalie* ("S. d'A."—
songe d'Athalie—Athalie's dream). Others of these notes are
worth quoting: "I thought of Glück. I played with two fingers.
Just the opposite of Lulli at the Théâtre Français, I added musical notes to Athalie's dream. I assumed a melody, attempted
to slow down, to retard (this is written in Italian—"ritardare"),
to connect, to cut off, to intervene—to conclude, to resolve—and
this in the meaning as well as the sound." (*Cahiers*, vol. 6, pp.
508–509—quoted in *Œuvres*, II, p. 1615.

All this gives us interesting insights into Valéry's attitude with
regard to composing a poem and some suggestions as to his
method of work at the time. But what of the accomplishment?
Is *La Jeune Parque* analogous to a recitative of Glück? Can there
be any real relation between them beyond an imaginative analogy? I doubt it.

The effect of the verses of Racine upon Valéry is a more tangi-
ble matter. Comparisons can be made on this point. That Valéry,
from this period on, admired Racine and would have liked to
write "Racinian" verses can be established. As a young poet,
Valéry had not discovered Racine.[14] As we saw earlier, he was
recalcitrant to his secondary studies, and the author of *Phèdre*
constituted part of a course of study that he found boring. Thirty

years later, his attitude was different, as is shown by a letter of
1917 to André Fontainas:

Funny thing. The influence of one's children's studies. Having them
recite the dream of Athalie made me aware of unsuspected things—
which cleared up once for all the difficulties that were troubling me.
I didn't appreciate Racine (and it was quite late!) until I was aware
of the problems he must have had and the skill he showed in solving
them. (Quoted in *Œuvres*, I, p. 1623.)

Ten years later (1927), in his speech of acceptance to the
Académie Française, he dwelt in some detail upon his delayed
but all the more complete admiration of Racine:

I admired him as I could, as a man who had discovered him thirty
years after his schooling, a discovery occasioned by certain minute
and at the same time immense problems of the art of verse. This in-
comparable composer (*sic*) had appeared to my youth as merely an
instrument of public education, which fortunately at that time took
good care not to teach us to like anything. I do not regret that long
period of misapprehension and that tardy acquaintance. We never can
judge a great man more exactly than by an immediate comparison
of his strength with our weaknesses. If circumstances offer us a certain difficulty and he has already conquered a similar one, we marvel
at the way he has untied the knot, made the obstacle vanish, and we
measure with the greatest and most deeply-felt precision that power
which triumphed, in comparison with ours which was ineffectual.
(*Œuvres*, I, p. 738.)

How "Racinian" are the verses of *La Jeune Parque*? Evidently
the obscurity is not Racinian, nor, more specifically, is one of the
causes of that obscurity: the twisting of the meaning of words
to fit a special case. The following is an example: "Va! je n'ai
plus besoin de ta race naïve, / Cher Serpent . . ." (v. 50–51)
(Go on! I no longer need your naïve race, / Dear Serpent . . .)
According to an excellent commentator, Jacques Duchesne-Guillemin, "race" here means "forme" or "corps." [15]
The flow of the alexandrines has certainly, at least in some
passages of *La Jeune Parque*, a quality not too different from
Racine (or the La Fontaine of *Adonis* or "Songe d'un habitant
du Mogol"). The young Fate's invocation to the stars (verses

18–27) has been compared to the prayer of Esther, in the tragedy of the same name:

> Tout-puissants étrangers, inévitables astres
> Qui daignez faire luire au lointain temporel
> Je ne sais quoi de pur et de surnaturel;
> Vous qui dans les mortels plongez jusques aux larmes
> Ces souverains éclats, ces invincibles armes,
>
> Et les élancements de votre éternité,
> Je suis seule avec vous, tremblante, ayant quitté
> Ma couche; et sur l'écueil mordu par la merveille,
> J'interroge mon cœur quelle douleur l'éveille,
> Quel crime par moi-même ou sur moi consommé? . . .

(All-powerful strangers, inevitable stars / Who deign to cause to shine in the temporal distance / Something indescribably pure and supernatural; / You who into mortals plunge so as to cause tears / Those sovereign outbursts, those invincible arms, / And the projections of your eternity, / I am alone with you and trembling, having left / My bed; and on the reef bitten by the marvel, / I ask my heart what grief wakens it, / What crime by myself or on myself committed? . . .)

Several expressions in these verses are not at all Racinian: "in-évitables astres," "au lointain temporel," "sur l'écueil mordu par la merveille." But most of the passage does have a Racinian or seventeenth-century quality.

Having discussed in some detail the genesis and the sources of *La Jeune Parque*, I shall now approach the poem itself. The subject, the real subject, is decidedly abstract: thought conscious of itself. As Valéry defined it, in a more complicated way, to Frédéric Lefèvre:

The real subject of the poem is the depiction of a succession of psychological substitutions, and, in short, the changes of a consciousness during the passage of a night. I tried my best, at the cost of an unbelievable struggle, to express the modulation of a life. But our psychological language is extremely poor. I had to impoverish it further, since the majority of the words that make it up are incompatible with a poetic tone. . . . (*Œuvres*, I, p. 1613.)

In a long letter of 1917 to the Belgian poet, Albert Mockel, he pointed out that he had expressed the subject "rather clearly in fragments which I suppressed because of not being able to get them right. . . . Too hard: the verses were impossible, dry, brittle as dry bones, or irremediably flat. In order to soften the poem a bit, I had to insert passages not planned before and written later. All that is sexual is an addition. For instance, the passage near the middle, on Spring, which now seems of essential importance." (*Œuvres*, I, p. 1621.)

The main subject of the poem being too abstract, he had therefore to introduce a secondary subject, which is the story of *La Jeune Parque* (the young Fate), a young woman faced with two problems: love and death. The title comes from this second subject, since the word "fate" evokes destiny rather than thought. To attempt to give a resumé of the "autobiography" (which is what Valéry called the poem in a letter to Gide: June 14, 1917— *Corresp.* Gide-Valéry, p. 448) of the consciousness of a young woman is very difficult, if not impossible. One of the best commentators, Jacques Duchesne-Guillemin, attempted, in his *Essai sur la Jeune Parque*,[16] a "canevas chronologique" of the poem, an effort to show, step by step, what Valéry called "the succession of psychological substitutions" that make up this work. The commentary divides *La Jeune Parque* into sixteen numbered sections. It distinguishes two "acts," but there are also sections entitled "before the first act" and "between the acts." There are not only flashbacks—the part "before the first act" is verses 107–210 (itself divided into three sections)—and these are not necessarily a source of obscurity—but there are also what I call "contaminations," which are generally confusing. Thus, verses 102–210, the commentator's section 8, a part of which he calls "Act I," coincide though not completely, with sections 1, 2, and 3, verses 107–210, which make up the part called "before the first act." I take this to mean that the "autobiographical" narration in these verses is hovering in between past and present and possibly confusing the two.

I shall now attempt my own simplified resumé of the poem, basing it upon Duchesne-Guillemin's analysis, but avoiding the complications of his "chronological canvas." The poem opens with the anguished awakening of a young woman, the "Young

Fate." She has a certain resemblance to Psyché. In fact, Valéry
had thought, at one point, of entitling the poem *Psyché*, but had
decided against it, partly because his friend, Pierre Louÿs, was
writing a novel (never to be finished) with that title. The quotation used as epigraph to the poem: "Did Heaven form that
mass of marvels to be the dwelling of a serpent" is a quotation
from Corneille's *Psyché;* and early in Valéry's poem occurs the
section known as the "Serpent" (the heroine feels the bite of a
serpent). Let me recall that in the *Legend of Cupid and Psyché*,
Psyché's unknown lover, who turns out to be Cupid, is said by
her jealous friends to be a serpent. Here the serpent symbolizes
the Young Fate's sexual desires. As she comes slowly to consciousness, in a setting of a starry night on the seashore, she is
in a state of confusion between the desire for love and that for
sublimation in death. Verses 209–210, obscure but important,
since they are enclosed by quotations marks in most editions
(and, in the *Œuvres* they are capitalized), have been interpreted
as meaning that the Young Fate wishes to escape from her mortal
condition and become equal to the gods: "Que dans le ciel placés,
mes yeux tracent mon temple! / Et que sur moi repose un autel
sans example!" (In heaven placed would that my eyes trace my
temple! / And that upon me there rest an altar without example!)
But the Young Fate feels the temptation of the "secret sister"
(the sensual side of her being), that "burns" within her (v. 48–
49) and she recalls how, with the coming of spring, love makes
a strong appeal:

> L'étonnant printemps rit, viole . . . On ne sait d'où
> Venu? Mais la candeur ruisselle à mots si doux
> Qu'une tendresse prend la terre à ses entrailles . . .
>
> Quelle résisterait, mortelle, à ces remous?
> Quelle mortelle?
>   Moi, si pure, mes genoux
> Pressentent les terreurs de genoux sans défense . . .
> Mon cœur bat! mon cœur bat! mon sein brûle et m'entraîne! . . .
>   (verses 227–229, 243–245, 254.)

(Surprising spring laughs, violates . . . From one knows not
where / Come? But its candor flows with such sweet words /
That tenderness seizes the entrails of the earth . . .

Who could resist as a mortal this agitation? / What mortal woman? I so pure, my knees / Portend the terrors of defenseless knees . . .

My heart beats! my heart beats! my breast burns and carries me away! . . .)

What Duchesne-Guillemin calls the "Second Act" begins with verse 325: "Mystérieuse мог." It is the dawn. The Young Fate has a vision of islands: a brilliant passage, often quoted:

> Salut! Divinités par la rose et le sel,
> Et les premiers jouets de la jeune lumière,
> Iles! . . . Ruches bientôt, quand la flamme première
> Fera que votre roche, îles que je prédis,
> Ressente en rougissant de puissants paradis;
> Cimes qu'un feu féconde à peine intimidées,
> Bois qui bourdonnerez de bêtes et d'idées,
> D'hymnes d'hommes comblés des dons du juste éther,
> Iles! dans la rumeur des ceintures de mer,
> Mères vierges toujours, même portant ces marques,
> Vous m'êtes à genoux de merveilleuses Parques:
> Rien n'égale dans l'air les fleurs que vous placez,
> Mais, dans la profondeur, que vos pieds sont glacés!
>
> (verses 348–360.)

(Hail, divinities by means of rose and salt, / And the first playthings of the young light, / Islands! . . . Hives soon, when the first flame / Will cause your rock, islands that I predict, / To feel while blushing powerful paradises; / Peaks which a fire enlivens hardly intimidated, / Woods which will hum with beasts and ideas, / And with hymns of men who have been favored by gifts of the just empyrean, / Islands! in the rustle of the girdles of the sea, / Mothers still virgins, even bearing these marks, / Kneeling you are for me marvelous Fates: / Nothing in the air equals the flowers you place there, / But, in the depths, how frozen are your feet!)

Finally the sun appears, and the poem ends with the Young Fate accepting life.

La Jeune Parque was, oddly enough, a success. The 600 copies of the first edition sold out rapidly. The influential critic of *Le Temps,* Paul Souday, devoted to the poem the whole of his literary *feuilleton* of June 28, 1917. One might question how many of the buyers of the volume read it through and how many of these made head or tail of it, but there is no doubt of the fact that, with the publication of *La Jeune Parque* in June, 1917, Paul Valéry passed from obscurity to the forefront, not only of French poetry, but of French literature in general.

III   *Poetic "Exercises"*

The long and arduous "exercise" constituted by the writing of *La Jeune Parque* did not exhaust the poetic vein of Paul Valéry; on the contrary—it proved a stimulus to further production. During the months when he was completing his long poem and in the months and years following its publication (especially between 1917 and 1922), he wrote a considerable number (twenty-five to thirty, maybe more) poems of varying lengths and types, which he published, first in a wide variety of magazines, then republished (most of them) in the volume, *Charmes,* the first edition of which appeared in June, 1922. The complete title of this volume was *Charmes, ou poèmes* (the French word *charmes* comes from the Latin *carmina,* songs or poems). Also in this period a group of his early poems (almost all revised, as I said earlier) was finally published in volume form, but not by Gallimard. It was entitled *Album de vers anciens* and was printed in 1920 by Adrienne Monnier.

As to the connection between the effort expended in composing *La Jeune Parque* and the outburst of inspiration represented by the poems of *Charmes,* Valéry commented on this a number of times. For instance, he said to Frédéric Lefèvre:

This labor of four years taught me, I believe, many things of which I didn't even have the faintest inkling. It seems to me that to clarify one's ideas there is nothing like writing a long, obscure poem. Having finished the poem, I composed almost immediately and with free-flowing inspiration, *Aurore* and *Palme,* as if the severity and the length of my effort were recompensed by a lightness and an ease which can come only after a training period rigorous and grimly determined upon. . . . (Quoted in *Œuvres,* I, p. 1613.)

The majority of these poems were written or begun (this was the case of the "Cimetière marin" and the "Fragments du Narcisse") in the last two years of the War. "Aurore" and "Palme," originally one poem, date from the summer of 1917. In the following summer, with the German advance threatening Paris, (it was not halted until late July), Edouard Lebey left the capital for an estate in Normandy, near Avranches, and took his secretary with him. Valéry found the château of L'Isle-Manière ugly, but the domain was beautiful—lush vegetation and magnificent trees—and this proved a source of inspiration. Four poems, "Le Rameur," "Au Platane," "La Pythie," [17] and "La Fausse Morte," were written here.

As I said above, the poems collected in the volume *Charmes* vary greatly in subject-matter,[18] in form and in size: from eight- or ten-verse impressions, such as "Intérieur" and "La Fausse Morte," to the extensive development of the "Fragments du Narcisse," which in the final version came to 314 verses. The variety of the verse forms used in *Charmes* is worth noting: Valéry, as we know, attached great importance to the element of form. With the exception of the first poem, "Aurore," and the last, "Palme," which were, as I said, originally one poem, and "Les Pas" and "Ode secrète," which have the same stanza form, (octosyllabic quatrain, riming *abab*) but differ in length, each poem of the twenty-one included differs in form.

There are three regular odes: two, "Aurore" and "Palme," in heptasyllabic dizains and one, "La Pythie," in octosyllabic dizains. "Ebauche d'un serpent" is also in octosyllabic dizains, but has an irregular rime scheme. There are five sonnets, two of them regular, but one of these ("La Dormeuse") is in alexandrines, the other ("L'Abeille") is octosyllabic. "Les Grenades" and "Le Vin perdu" are irregularly-rimed octosyllabic sonnets, while "Le Sylphe" is an irregularly-rimed sonnet in five-syllable verse. In 1896, Valéry had written an exquisite *quatorzain* ("Vue"); *Charmes* contains another, as exquisite and much less obscure: "La Ceinture."

Seven poems are in quatrains, with five of these riming regularly *abab*: "Le Rameur" in alexandrines; "Les Pas" and "Ode secrète" are octosyllabic but of different lengths; "Poésie" is in verses of six syllables, and in "Au Platane" alexandrines alternate with verses of six syllables. "Cantique des colonnes" in verses of six syllables and "L'Insinuant" in verses of five, have irregular rime schemes. One other poem in strophes, "Le Cimetière marin," is in sizains, riming *aabccb*.

The short "Intérieur" is in alexandrines riming *aabb*, etc., while the slightly longer "La Fausse Morte" is mostly in alexandrines and *rimes plates*. "Fragments du Narcisse" has the alexandrines and *rimes plates* characteristic of narrative and dramatic poetry, with a few shorter verses and occasional irregularities in the rime scheme.

It will be impossible here to cite or to comment on all of the twenty-one poems of *Charmes*, though the large majority deserve such treatment. I recommend to the reader the enlightening but discreet and sober commentaries and notes of Robert Monestier, in the Classiques Larousse edition of *Charmes*. Examples will have to suffice here. As an example of the shorter pieces, "La Ceinture":

LA CEINTURE

Quand le ciel couleur d'une joue
Laisse enfin les yeux le chérir
Et qu'au point doré de périr
Dans les roses le temps se joue,

Devant le muet de plaisir
Qu'enchaîne une telle peinture,
Danse une Ombre à libre ceinture
Que le soir est près de saisir.

Cette ceinture vagabonde
Fait dans le souffle aérien
Frémir le suprême lien
De mon silence avec ce monde . . .

Absent, présent. . . . Je suis bien seul,
Et sombre, ô sauve linceul.

(*Œuvres*, I, p. 121.
© *Editions Gallimard*.)

(THE GIRDLE. When the sky colored like a cheek / Finally allows the eyes to cherish it / And when at the golden point of perishing / Time plays in the roses, / Before the silent pleasure / Chained by such a painting, / Dances a shadow with a free girdle / Which the evening is ready to seize. / This vagabond girdle / Causes in the airy breath / To tremble the supreme bond / Of my silence with this world . . . / Absent, present . . . I am really alone, / And sombre, O suave shroud.)

Among the longer pieces, "Fragments du Narcisse," reviving the theme and incorporating some portions of one of the best of the early poems, contains some of the most exquisite verses written by Valéry. In his discussion (in 1941) of his poems on the Narcissus myth (referred to above, pages 9–10), he spoke of the genesis of this poem:

A rather long time later the idea came to me to write a sort of counterpart to that so severe and obscure poem, *La Jeune Parque*. I chose— or rather it chose itself—that Narcissus theme which I had used before—a theme suitable for what I wanted to create, that is, a work which would be almost the opposite of *La Jeune Parque*, far simpler in its form and creating almost no difficulty of comprehension, with my effort being concentrated especially on the harmony of the language itself. (Quoted in *Œuvres,* I, p. 1661.)

His success in this effort was considerable. He himself felt that verses 48–55 of Part I were the most perfect he had ever written:

> O douceur de survivre à la force du jour,
> Quand elle se retire enfin rose d'amour,
> Encore un peu brûlante, et lasse, mais comblée,
> Et de tant de trésors tendrement accablée
> Par de tels souvenirs qu'ils empourprent sa mort,
> Et qu'ils la font heureuse agenouiller dans l'or,
> Puis s'étendre, se fondre, et perdre sa vendange,
> Et s'éteindre en un songe en qui le soir se change.
>   (*Œuvres,* I, p. 123.)

(How sweet to survive the force of the day, / When it at length withdraws rosy with love, / Still a bit burning and tired, but fulfilled, / And tenderly overwhelmed with so many treasures / With such memories that they empurple its death, / And they make it happily kneel in gold, / Then stretch out, melt and lose its harvest, / And die out in the dream into which evening changes.)

"The eight verses you quote there," he said to Jean de Latour, who in 1935 had written an *Examen de Valéry*, "are very exactly those which cost me the most effort and which I consider to be the most perfect of all I have written. I mean most in conformity to what I wished them to be, bound by all the constraints which I had ordained for them. Note that, otherwise, they are absolutely devoid of ideas and thus they attain that degree of purity which constitutes exactly what I call *pure poetry*." (Quoted in *Œuvres*, I, pp. 1661–1662.)

It is interesting to contrast the verses of "Narcisse parle," quoted in the first chapter, with the final form; for example: "J'entends l'herbe d'argent grandir dans l'ombre sainte" becomes "J'entends l'herbe des nuits croître dans l'ombre sainte."

The first eleven verses of Part II of the "Fragments" have been often quoted and are justly admired:

> Fontaine, ma fontaine, eau froidement présente,
> Douce aux purs animaux, aux humains complaisante
> Qui d'eux-mêmes tentés suivent au fond la mort,
> Tout est songe pour toi, Sœur tranquille du Sort!
> A peine en souvenir change-t-il un présage,
> Que pareille sans cesse à son fuyant visage,
> Sitôt de ton sommeil les cieux te sont ravis!
> Mais si pure tu sois des êtres que tu vis,
> Onde, sur qui les ans passent comme les nues,
> Que de choses pourtaint doivent t'être connues,
> Astres, roses, saisons, les corps et leurs amours!
>   (*Œuvres*, I, p. 126.)

(Fountain, my fountain, water coldly present, / Gentle to pure animals, to humans sympathetic / Who, themselves tempted, follow death in the depths, / All is a dream for thee, tranquil Sister of Fate! / Scarcely into a memory does it change a foreshadowing, / Then ceaselessly similar to its fleeting face, / At once the skies of thy sleep are ravished from thee! / But pure as you may be of the beings you have seen, / Fount, over whom the years pass like the clouds, / How many things must yet be known to thee, / Stars, roses, seasons, bodies and their loves!)

Valéry never completed these "Fragments." As he said in 1926: "Leisure, the necesary inclination, the strength, the patience to do the job are lacking and will be lacking." (*Œuvres,* I, p. 1662.) The *Cantate du Narcisse,* written in 1938 to be set to music by Germaine Tailleferre, is an entirely different work and of much less interest.

The best-known and *one* of the best, if not the best, of Valéry's poems, "Le Cimetière marin," appeared in *Charmes,* after having been published in the *Nouvelle Revue française,* June 1, 1920. It shortly took its place in the mind of the cultivated general public as the *typical* obscure modern poem. It has since been reprinted, complete or in various mutilated ways, in countless anthologies, including school texts, the first of these being, as far as I know, the third volume of Marcel Braunschvicg's *Notre Littérature étudiée dans les textes* (1926), which published about one third of the poem. An American anthology, Régis Michaud's *Vingtième Siècle* (which was far ahead of its time and had little success) published the poem in 1933.

This poem has been analyzed and dissected in the minutest detail by a host of commentators and exegetes. The best-known of these exegeses is that of Gustave Cohen[19], who in 1928 devoted a Sorbonne course to the poem. It was later published in a volume of many (small) pages. Valéry was present at the first lecture of Cohen's course, and, in his important essay on the poem and on his conception of poetry in general (which first appeared in the *Nouvelle Revue française,* March 1, 1933, and later served as a preface to Cohen's book), he wrote of his feelings on that occasion. His feelings were complex:

I felt as if I was my own Shade. . . . I felt like a captured shade; and yet I identified myself at moments with some one of those students who were following attentively and were taking notes, and who, from time to time, smiled at that shade whose poem was being read and commented on, stanza by stanza.

I admit that *in my quality of student* I had little reverence for the poet—isolated, exposed and embarrassed in his seat. My presence was strangely divided into several ways of being there. In this diversity of feelings . . . the dominant one was the sense of contrast between the memory of my work, a memory which was now being revived, and the finished appearance, the determined and fixed work to which M. Cohen's analysis was being applied. (*Œuvres,* I, pp. 1498–1499.)

Valéry went on to speak very courteously and very kindly of
the exactness and completeness of Cohen's commentary:

While listening to M. Cohen as he read the strophes of my text and
gave to each its definite meaning and its place in the development, I
was divided between the satisfaction of seeing that the intentions and
expressions of a poem held to be very obscure were here perfectly
understood and expounded—and the strange, almost painful feeling to
which I have alluded. (*Œuvres*, I, p. 1499.)

Further on, he gave additional credit to Cohen's exposé:

I wrote a "score,"—but I can "hear" it only when executed by the soul
and mind of someone else. That is why M. Cohen's work . . . is
singularly precious to me. He discovered my intentions with a care
and a method that were remarkable, applying to a contemporary text
the same science and the same precision that he is accustomed to dis-
play in his learned studies of literary history. He retraced the architecture of the poem, and equally well he noted the details—pointing
out, for example, those recurrences of terms which reveal the tendencies characteristic of a mind. (*Œuvres*, I, pp. 1506–1507.)

Does this mean that Valéry felt that Cohen's exegesis of "Le
Cimetière marin" was perfect, irreproachable? Not necessarily.
Valéry was invariably courteous to his commentators and never
(at least in public) said "Your interpretation is ridiculous." It
was in reference to Alain's commentary of *Charmes* (1928) that
he said: "Mes vers ont le sens qu'on leur prête" (My verses have
the meaning that people attach to them). (*Œuvres*, I, p. 1509.)
But it was in the essay quoted from above, "Au sujet du 'Cimetière marin'", that he exposed most clearly his own feeling as to
the commentaries of his poems:

To sum up, the more a poem is in conformity to Poetry, the less is it
possible that it be thought in prose without perishing. . . . If I am
questioned . . . about what I "meant to say" in such and such a poem,
I reply that I didn't "mean to say" but that I "meant to do," and it
was the intention of "doing" that caused what I said. (*Œuvres*, I,
p. 1503.)

Therefore, neither the commentary of Alain or that of Gustave
Cohen nor that of Bernard Weinberg[20] (to name a few) is *the*

explanation of the poem. These particular commentators and others have read "Le Cimetière marin" with intuition and understanding and have made remarks that will help the general reader appreciate the poem, but it will be noted that these commentaries diverge on many points; and if the reader feels differently about details or about the poem in general, he has the right to do so.

Valéry was quite specific about the origin of the poem and his general intentions in writing it, not only in "Au sujet du 'Cimetière marin'", but more explicitly in his earlier (1926) *Entretiens aver Frédéric Lefèvre:*

I had written a few strophes of the "Cimetière marin" while I was composing *La Jeune Parque.* It was born, like most of my poems, from the unexpected presence in my mind of a certain rhythm. I was surprised, one morning, to find in my head decasyllabic verses. This type of verse was rarely used by French poets in the nineteenth century. . . . It is a verse difficult to handle because of the fact that it comes very easily. . . . As for the content of the poem, it is made up of memories of my native city. It is almost the only one of my poems into which I put something of my own life.

This cemetery exists. It dominates the sea, on which one sees the doves, that is the fishermen's boats, wandering and *pecking.* . . . That word scandalized people. Sailors say of a ship that plunges forward into a wave that it is sticking in its nose. The image is similar. It is obvious to any one who has been there. (*Œuvres*, I, pp. 1674–1675.)

Though for Valéry none of his poems was ever *really* finished, he was surely exaggerating somewhat when he said that the shape of this work was fixed by accident:

One afternoon of the year 1920, our late friend, Jacques Rivière, having come to visit me, found me working on a "version" of the "Cimetière marin," planning to take up here, to suppress there, to intervene here and there. . . . He insisted on seeing the poem, and having read it, he took it away. There is nothing more decisive then the mind of a magazine editor. It was thus by accident that the shape of this work was fixed. ("Au sujet du 'Cimetière marin,'" *Œuvres*, I, p. 1500.)

To state that the final form of the poem was fixed by accident is, in my opinion, a definite exaggeration. If Valéry had worked longer on the poem, there would have been modifications; he would have dropped some stanzas, added others, but the work as we have it gives evidence of being carefully organized and this organization would have been maintained. On a much smaller scale it seems to be structured as perfectly as *A la Recherche du temps perdu*. The opening stanza and the final stanza represent definitely a beginning and an end, with the image (surprising to the first readers but now known to everybody) of "ce toit tranquille" (this tranquil roof) reprised at the end, and the poem ending with a shock in the image "où picoraient des focs!" (where mainsails were pecking—"focs" is a technical nautical term).

It is not necessary to analyze in detail this well-known poem. Who has not seen the frequently-reproduced photograph of the Cemetery by the sea of Sète, with the Mediterranean shown above the tombs and the trees, making the comparison to a roof quite natural? And who has not wondered, like myself, about the expression "entre les pins palpite" (palpitates amid the pines), when the trees in the photograph are obviously cypresses? Did Paul Valéry's memory fail him (he had not returned to Sète for some years), or, as is more likely, did purely formal poetic considerations dictate the replacement of cypresses by pines? [21]

The poem, I repeat, is so well known that I hesitate to expatiate further on it. It is, to sum up, a successful example of a *poetic* meditation on *philosophic* themes: the immutable (the shimmering noonday sun on the Mediterranean), the changeable (the sea), man and death. But it also contains imagery of great richness and originality, not only philosophical but also, at times, sensual. And a rhythmic pattern that evolves naturally from the calm of the opening to the movement of the end: "Envolez-vous, pages tout éblouies . . ." (Fly away, dazzled pages . . .)

IV *Return to Prose: the Dialogues*

The period which I am treating, in which Paul Valéry reached the peak of his poetic production, saw him also make a brilliant entrance into another genre, the Socratic (or Platonic) dialogue. Two of the dialogues, *Eupalinos ou l'architecte* and *L'Ame et la danse*, were written (and published) in 1921. Both were *ouvrages de commande*. The first of these dialogues, one of Valéry's finest works, both in the perfection of its form and the significance of its ideas, is an impressive demonstration of the way in which the author of the "Cimetière marin" could attack a subject suggested to him by someone else and turn it into a masterpiece. He himself related, on a number of occasions, the origin of this dialogue. In May, 1923, he wrote to Paul Souday:

I was asked to write a text for the album *Architectures,* which is a collection of illustrations of buildings and architectural plans. This text was to be magnificently printed in an infolio, and had to be exactly adjusted to the decoration and the pagination of the work. I was therefore asked to make my contribution exactly 115,800 letters long, that is, 115,800 printed characters! It is true that these characters were to be sumptuous. I accepted. My dialogue was at first too long. I shortened it—and then, since it was a little too short, I lengthened it again. I finally found these requirements very interesting. But it may be that the text itself suffered a bit from all this. (*Lettres à quelques-uns,* p. 147.)

Another letter, over ten years later, to a certain Doutenville, pointed out why he chose the form of the dialogue:

This rigorous limitation (115,800 letters), at first surprising and annoying, but imposed upon a man more or less accustomed to poems in fixed forms, made me first reflect, then decide that the odd requirement proposed could be rather easily met by using the very elastic form of the dialogue. (An insignificant exchange of remarks, added or suppressed, permits one to fulfill the requirement of fixed, measured limits.) This adjustment was made easily on the proofs. (*Lettres à quelques-uns,* p. 214.)

The dialogue takes place in the underworld, between the shades of Socrates and his friend, Phædrus. The latter evokes the figure and the opinions of his former friend, the architect Eupalinos of Megara.[22] Eupalinos typifies *the* architect, practising an art, which, according to Socrates (and Valéry also) is the most complete, an art in which there are no *details*—that is, everything counts in the execution of a work of architecture. Phædrus relates how Eupalinos explained to him his theory of the three types of buildings: those that are *silent,* those that *speak,* and finally the highest type, those that *sing!* This leads by a natural transition to a comparison on the part of Socrates of the two supreme arts: architecture and music. After that comes the passage, referred to above, where Socrates describes the moment when he was at the parting of the ways and analyzes the meditations which caused him to choose to be a philosopher rather than an artist. The incident of the "ambiguous" object picked up on the seashore, described in detail by Socrates (preceded by a magnificent evocation of the Mediterranean seashore) recalls an incident of Valéry's youth, to which he alluded briefly in a letter of 1926[23] and at length in a *cahier* of 1916 (*Cahiers*, vol. 5, pp. 826–829.) His attitude, in 1916, toward this incident of 1887 or 1888 is shown by the title of a proposed subject of an essay: "Souvenirs de spéculations naïves." (*Loc. cit.*, p. 826.) A curious note in a *cahier* of 1912 shows with what distance and sense of proportion he was able to look upon his attitudes of twenty years earlier:

Do you recall the time when you were an angel! Angel without Christ I remember. It was a matter of look and will, the idea of running through everything with my eyes. I liked only fire. I believed that in the long run nothing could resist my scrutiny and my desire of scrutiny or rather I thought that someone could be like that and I had the clear and absolute idea that I was that one. Everything seemed to me so simple that literature had become impossible." (*Cahiers*, vol. 4, p. 705.)

To return to *Eupalinos*, Socrates felt that his meditations had led him in the wrong direction, and he regretted the artist he might have been. Did Valéry, in 1921, regret that he had made, in 1892, the same choice as Socrates? Note these verses in the "Cimetière marin" (which, I believe, have not hitherto been interpreted in this sense): "Après tant d'orgueil, après tant d'étrange / Oisiveté, mais pleine de pouvoir . . ." (After so much pride, after so long a strange / idleness but—an idleness—full of potential) (v. 32–33, *Œuvres*, I, p. 148.) Does this suggest that during his long period of poetic idleness, he felt that he had the potential of a great poet?

After weighing the pros and cons of this question, I reach the following conclusion: Valéry felt that the artist, the great artist, among whom the builder is the greatest, is superior to the mere thinker; the great Socrates regretted that he had sacrificed "construire" for "connaître." But I think also that Valéry was too modest to assimilate himself to Socrates; he hardly felt that he had been capable of becoming a supreme artist. For him, his own works (even at this period of most intense productivity) were not supreme construction, like a Greek temple; they were merely exercises. (See my discussion of this in Chapter V, part 4.)

The subject of *Eupalinos* shows that Valéry had not lost that interest in architecture manifested thirty years earlier. So far as the form of this dialogue is concerned, the necessity, referred to above, of filling a *specific* amount of space took its toll: the poet himself said, as we have seen: "It may be that the text suffered a bit from this." *Eupalinos* would have benefited by being shortened.

Most readers will agree that Valéry recaptured admirably the spirit (or what we now consider to be the spirit) of the dialogues of Plato. He himself was very modest—and frank about this: "I have never been in Greece, and, as for Greek, I was never anything but a very mediocre student, who gets lost reading Plato in the original, and who finds him, in translation, terribly long and often boring." [24]

Valéry indulged in other phases of literary activity in the years that I have been discussing. Since they form a part of the new rôle he was beginning to play in life, I shall consider them in the next chapter. A turning-point in Valéry's life came February 14, 1922, with the death of his employer. Edouard Lebey. He was thus unemployed, and while aware of the need of finding a new job, he really did not want to, as he said in a letter to André Gide eight months later: "It is strange to be out of a job, without the slightest desire to find one, without any taste for work, and thinking of tomorrow as we thought in 1913 of a War. Sense of the certainty of the impossible." (*Corresp. Gide-Valéry*, p. 491 —Letter of October 19, 1922.) We shall soon see that Paul Valéry's apprehensions as to his future were unwarranted.

CHAPTER 4

The Official Poet of France

I *Earning a Living*

BREAKING Paul Valéry's life into separate chapters, as I have done, is an oversimplification; the author of *Charmes* did not change overnight (between the death of his employer, February 14, 1922, and the next day) from a promising but never well-known and generally forgotten symbolist poet to the first poet of contemporary France. The mysterious process which led to the fame of Paul Valéry really began when he consented, in 1912, to the republication of his early poems. I call the process mysterious because I find it hard to explain. It was certainly not the result of a publicity campaign, and above all it was not the result of a conscious effort on the part of Valéry. Later, it is true—from the mid-twenties on—the poet's multiple activities kept his name before the public. Factors that contributed to his fame were publication by and in the *Nouvelle Revue française,* which had rapidly become preponderantly influential in the field of twentieth-century French literature, and the praise that he received from the powerful critic, Paul Souday. Another factor, maybe minor, was the public reading of his poems, beginning in 1919 in Adrienne Monnier's bookshop. Whatever may have been the cause, Paul Valéry received the consecration—in March, 1921, over a year before the publication of *Charmes*—of winning the competition organized by the review *Connaissance:* "Who is the greatest contemporary French poet?"

When Valéry received the news of this, he wrote politely to the review: "This astonishing bit of news which you have so kindly communicated to me fills me with melancholy as for myself and with regrets for the other poets, innocent victims. . . ." (Quoted in *Œuvres,* II, p. 1487.) Later, the same year, he wrote to Paul Claudel: "I want to tell you how much I was shocked by the imbecilic plebiscite of *la Connaissance.*" (*Œuvres,* II, p.

1486.) But was he *really* so displeased? Let me recall that, as early as 1912, he had worried about the possibility of finding himself "tomorrow" in a very "embarrassing" situation, and felt that if a book had been published it would "help." Now in 1921 he might have felt that fame (even if he sincerely believed that it was unjustified) would "help." And it did.

In the early twenties it was not only Valéry's fame as a poet that soared, he also obtained a growing reputation as an original and profound thinker, even a prophet. We saw earlier that the re-publication, in 1915, of his article of 1897, "Une Conquête allemande," provided a foundation for the prophetic career of this poet. In April, 1919, the English review, the *Athenæum,* published, under the heading, "Letter from France," an article entitled "The Spiritual Crisis." This was the English translation of a brief essay by Paul Valéry, the original of which was published four months later in the *Nouvelle Revue française* with the title "La Crise de l'esprit." This essay was widely read, soon became well known, and portions of it, especially the first sentence, were frequently quoted. Some people went so far as to declare that in the five pages of this essay Valéry said as much as—and more profoundly and effectively than—what was said in Spengler's lengthy *Decline of the West,* which had created quite a stir at about that time:

We civilizations, we now know that we are mortal.

We had heard tell of worlds completely disappeared, of empires sunk to the bottom with all their men and all their machines; descended into the unexplorable depths of the centuries with their gods and their laws. . . . We perceived through the density of history the phantoms of immense ships which had been laden with riches and intellect. We could not count them. But, after all, these wrecks were not our concern.

Elam, Nineveh, Babylon were vaguely beautiful names, and the total ruin of these worlds had as little meaning for us as their very existence. But *France, England, Russia* . . . they would also be beautiful names. *Lusitania* is also a fine name. And now we see that the abyss of history is deep enough for everybody. We feel that a civilization has the same fragility as a life. The circumstances that would send the works of Keats and those of Baudelaire to join the works of Menander are no longer inconceivable: they are in the newspapers. (*Œuvres,* I, p. 988.)

This brilliant essay, of which the gist is to be found in the preceding quotation, is an indication that Valéry's practice of daily cultivation of his brain, his daily habit for twenty-five years or more, had borne fruit. He had the ability to think things through. He once said: "From what have I suffered the most? Perhaps from the habit of developing my whole thought, of going right up to the end in myself." [1]

On numerous occasions in the succeeding years, Valéry was to give perfect expression to profound thoughts. Most strikingly perhaps in the four inscriptions formulated in 1937 for the newly-constructed Palais de Chaillot. No one has given a better expression of the significance and the function of a museum than Valéry did in these inscriptions, which I translate here:

"In these walls consecrated to marvels I welcome and preserve the works of the prodigious hand of the artist, equal and rival of his thought. The one is nothing without the other.

"It depends upon the one who passes here whether I am a tomb or a treasure, whether I speak or remain silent. It lies within your hands, friend. Enter not without desire.

"Every man creates without knowing it, just as he breathes. But the artist is aware of himself creating. His act engages his whole being. His beloved effort fortifies him.

"Rare things, beautiful things, here skillfully assembled, teach the eye to look upon as if never before seen all things which exist in the world." [2]

The unemployed Paul Valéry of 1922 solved very satisfactorily the problem of earning his living, though he did not actually get a "job" until July, 1933, when he was appointed to the position of administrator of the newly-created Centre Universitaire Méditerranéen at Nice. Four years later, he obtained a second "job," the position of professor of Poetics at the Collège de France. As for the period in between, I do not know whether our poet's course of action in the years following the death of Edouard Lebey was a carefully planned campaign or not. To make one's living as a writer, the surest method is to write best-selling novels, and the surest way to make novels sell well is (in France) to win a literary prize, especially the Prix Goncourt. But Valéry knew well that he would never be a best-selling novelist. What he did (did he choose to do it?) was to keep his name constantly

in the eyes of the literary public. He wrote unceasingly—
ouvrages de commande of all sorts, including many prefaces;
he was co-editor of a fine literary quarterly; he lectured, in Paris,
in the provinces, all over Europe (but never in America) on a
wide variety of subjects; he published numberless deluxe bro-
chures, pamphlets, small volumes designed to become collectors'
items; he dedicated memorials and monuments; he presided over
conferences and conventions; he succeeded in obtaining official
honors: the Académie Française (1925), the Legion of Honor—
chevalier, 1923, *officier*, 1926, *commandeur*, 1931.

The details of these activities have been faithfully related by
Agathe Rouart-Valéry in her *Introduction biographique*. I shall
make no effort to reproduce this, and shall limit myself to a
general examination of the poet's career during this period, with
an extended discussion of some highlights.

It has been said that Paul Valéry's rôle as co-editor of the
quarterly *Commerce* was mainly that of a figurehead. This handsome publication, with its aggressively antiliterary title, listed
three co-editors: Paul Valéry, Valery Larbaud and Léon-Paul
Fargue.[3] Twenty-nine numbers were published between 1924
and 1932. It was subsidized by Marguerite Caetani, Princess
Bassiano. This American wife of an Italian Prince devoted her
considerable wealth throughout her life to the cause of good
literature. It has been said that Paul Valéry was not too active
as editor of *Commerce*, but it served at least as a means of publication for him; during its eight years of existence and its twenty-
nine issues, it published about a dozen of his works.

It must be admitted that, though as I said he wrote constantly,
after 1922 Valéry did not write any poetry of very great significance. The author of the "Cimetière marin" wrote, in the last
twenty years of his life, verse in *quantity* comparable to his three
published volumes of poetry (I am referring to the *Album de
vers anciens, La Jeune Parque* and *Charmes*), but it was hardly
more than competent versifying: the texts of the ballets *Amphion*
and *Sémiramis* (these two in free verse), the *Cantate du Narcisse*
and the translation of Virgil's *Bucolics* (this last in blank
verse.)[4]

A part of Valéry's program of keeping his name constantly
before the eyes of the literary world was the publication of many
small, deluxe volumes. A number of these were formed of se-

lected extracts from his *cahiers*. The first to be published, *Cahier B 1910* (1924), was merely the reproduction of a *cahier* written in 1910. Later (1926 and 1927) he issued under the enigmatic titles of *Rhumbs* and *Autre Rhumbs*[5] selected extracts from many *cahiers* of various dates, classified according to the subject-matter. These fragments, which along with several other similar small volumes, were collected, shortly before the poet's death in two volumes entitled *Tel Quel;* this is first-class Valéry, but it should be remembered that it was written earlier, most of it *much* earlier.

As far as literary events in the life of Paul Valéry are concerned, the most important, during the twenties, that is, after the publication of *Charmes* in June, 1922, were the appearance, in June, 1924, of the collection of prose writings entitled *Variété*, and the "Discours de réception à l'Académie française," given June 23, 1927, and printed in *Le Temps* the next day. *Variété*, the first of five collections bearing that title, contained all of Valéry's significant prose writings up to that date, with the exception of the *Soirée avec Monsieur Teste* and "Une Conquête allemande" (also entitled "Une Conquête méthodique" and republished under that title in volume form at about the same date as *Variété*). The impact of these essays, for the first time available to the general public in convenient form, was considerable. I have already commented on two of these, the "Introduction à la méthode de Léonard de Vinci" (Chapter 2—but see also Chapter 7, part II,) and "La Crise de l'esprit" (Chapter 4). Four other essays are of great interest. "Au sujet d'*Euréka*," which I mentioned in my first chapter, reveals Valéry's enthusiasm for and his debt to Poe. "Avant-propos à la *Connaissance de la déesse*," the preface to a collection of poems by Lucien Fabre, a poet now completely forgotten, consists of a defense of symbolism and an excellent exposé of Valéry's theory of "pure" poetry. "Au sujet d'*Adonis*" contained, in addition to a justifiable rehabilitation of La Fontaine's forgotten poem, an eloquent presentation of Valéry's theory of the importance in poetry of form—strict and rigorous form.

"Variations sur une pensée" surprised, indeed shocked, many readers. Speaking of the famous *pensée* of Pascal, "le silence éternel de ces espaces infinis m'effraie," Valéry said this is a perfect *poem*, but it is not at all a *thought*. Thinkers and philosophers, from the Greeks, from the author of the *Psalms* to Immanuel Kant, says Valéry, have proclaimed that "the Heavens declare the glory of God and the firmament showeth his handiwork" or have seen in those infinite but starry spaces "the army of inalterable law." Not so Pascal, who claims to be frightened. (*Œuvres*, I, pp. 459–471.) Now among French writers, thinkers, philosophers, Pascal, even more than Racine, has been an untouchable. One could say of him, as Wordsworth of Shakespeare: "Other abide our question; thou art free!" Attacking Pascal was almost like attacking Santa Claus! But this was not a passing whim on the part of Valéry; his *cahiers* show him to have been consistently anti-Pascal.

II *Glory*

Election to the Académie française has rarely been done on the basis of pure merit, at least during the twentieth century. A candidate must proclaim his candidacy, and even indicate the chair to which he is seeking to be elected. He must also make formal visits to all members, soliciting their support. As early as the spring of 1923, Valéry was encouraged—by the diplomat and historian, Gabriel Hanotaux—to be a candidate for the chair of Delcassé, who had just died. But it was a year and a half later (November 21, 1924) that he announced his candidacy for the chair of the Comte d'Haussonville. In the following year, the author of the "Cimetière marin" made his academic visits, including of course the marshalls, Joffre and Foch. He was on good terms with the latter, who, shortly before the election, advised him to shift his candidacy to the chair of Anatole France, who had died the year before. This tactic was successful, and Paul Valéry was elected November 19, 1925. He described how, while the election was taking place, he was correcting proof for a new edition of *La Jeune Parque* at the same table at which he had worked on the poem ten years before. Anxious to know the result, he walked down to the banks of the Seine, where he was told the good news by the academician René Boylesve (who was to die two months later). (*Œuvres*, I, p. 49.)

Valéry had to wait nineteen months before being officially received into the august body. He himself designed the hilt of his sword (an essential part of the traditional academic costume), including in it a young woman of Greek appearance

who undoubtedly represented the "Jeune Parque" and a serpent.
When he sent a photograph of himself in his costume to a friend,
he humorously explained: "The enclosed photo offers you a diplomat or a prefect. Don't be afraid. It's the effigy of a costume.
As is fitting, the head is of no importance." [6]

It is customary for a *Discours de réception* to consist of the
eulogy of one's predecessor in the chair. At the time of his death
Anatole France still enjoyed a high reputation. In 1924, if the
literary public in the United States had been asked to name the
greatest contemporary French writer, I am sure Anatole France
would have been chosen. In France his fame may have diminished somewhat since 1914, but possibly for political reasons:
France was a pacifist in 1914, and later he expressed sympathy
for Communism. That, after his death, he had received what one
might call the "consecration" of a violent attack by the surrealists
in a pamphlet entitle *Un Cadavre* ("Have you ever slapped a
corpse?" queried Aragon) was more or less the indication that
he was still a national figure. The eulogy of Anatole France
would therefore be expected to be something more than the
perfunctory praise accorded to any nonentity.

Valéry began his speech with a graceful tribute to the late
Boylesve (not quite a nonentity; his second-rate novels are still
pleasantly readable) who, you will recall, had kindly informed
Valéry of his election. Then the new Academician began a discussion of literary trends in the nineties and soon embarked upon
an examination of the writer whom he never once mentioned
by name, but referred to as his "illustrious predecessor." The
closest he came to naming the name was in the sentence: "He
himself was hardly possible or conceivable except in France, of
which he took the name." (*Œuvres*, I, p. 729.) This discourse,
often couched in mild irony and consisting of rather detailed
literary analysis and criticism aimed at explaining a phenomenon,
was possibly shocking to some listeners, who expected the conventional eulogy. Reread forty years later, it appears in no way
a diatribe but a rather sound and moderate if somewhat abstract
judgment of a writer for whom Paul Valéry's first reaction had
been scorn.

He never forgave Anatole France for the incident of *L'Après-
midi d'un faune*. In 1874, Mallarmé endeavored to have his poem
published in the third instalment of the collection of poetry en-

titled *Le Parnasse contemporain.* The first instalment, in 1866, had contained a whole group of his poems; the second, in 1871, had published the "Scène" from *Hérodiade.* Mallarmé was thus a charter member of the Parnasse group and had every reason to assume that an important poem offered by him would be accepted. But, in 1874, the editorial committee for the volume included—in addition to François Coppée and Théodore de Banville, charming men (if not very good poets, especially the former) and good friends of Mallarmé—Anatole France. France was then unkown as a writer, but had somehow reached a position of prestige. In any case he outvoted Coppée and Banville (he presumably had the most influence with the publisher, Alphonse Lemerre) and turned down Mallarmé's poem, saying "if we published it, people would laugh at us." [7] It is Anatole France that people laugh at, for his mistake in judgment was as ludicrous as it was inexcusable.

III *The Unexpected Dramatist*

Valéry is usually not thought of as a dramatist, though his ballets and his *Cantate du Narcisse* were written in the dramatic form. His biographer informs us that in 1887 he wrote two little plays: *Le Rêve de Morgan* and *Les Esclaves.* (*Œuvres,* I, p. 15.) The manuscript of these was exhibited in 1956. [8] Later he planned but never wrote a tragedy on the Emperor Tiberius: *Tibère ou la Raison couronnée.* [9] He would have been rather surprised, I imagine, to learn that two of his later works, one of them not written as a play, were to be staged, with considerable success, in the Paris of the sixties. [10] I am referring to the dialogue, *L'Idée fixe* (1932) and the unfinished play, *Mon Faust* (written in 1940, first published in 1941).

L'Idée fixe, ou deux hommes à la mer is a dialogue between a doctor and a person who, toward the middle, names himself "Edmond T . . ." and who therefore must be none other than our old friend, Monsieur Teste. I find it impossible to state precisely what is the subject of this dialogue. It is certainly not "l'idée fixe," for near the beginning Edmond T . . . asserts that *idées fixes* do not and cannot exist. What was surely Valéry's intent was to compose a dialogue of ideas (possibly somewhat analogous to the *Neveu de Rameau* and the *Rêve de d'Alembert* of Diderot [11]) in which two brilliant thinkers, whose principal interest seems to be the physiological and psychological study of man and his capacities, toss ideas—like balls—back and forth, passing with bewildering facility from one subject to another. It is dazzling and fascinating, and it is surely a byproduct, the best published byproduct, of the years of meditation on man's intellect and his faculties that are noted down in the *cahiers*.

Paul Valéry began to make notes on what he called the "third" *Faust* at least as early as the summer of 1924. (*Cahiers*, vol. 10, p. 137.) The first mention of "IIIe Faust" as such is in a *cahier* of November, 1926: "Der 3me Faust. Fantaisie. Méphisto et Faust à l'opéra de Vienne.[12] Crép. des dieux. M. Je te rajeunirai encore une fois! F. Mais si bien que rien n'aura eu lieu . . ." (*Cahiers*, vol. 11, p. 814.) (The 3rd Faust. Fantasy. Mephisto and Faust at the Vienna opera. Twilight of the gods. M. I will rejuvenate you once more! F. But so well that nothing will ever have happened . . .) Numerous other notes headed "IIIe Faust" occur in the years following in the *cahiers*.

The work which was published under the title of *Mon Faust* (*ébauches*) was written in the tragic summer of 1940, which Valéry spent with his family at Dinard in Brittany. During the dramatic events of 1914 and 1915, the act of revising his early poems and working on *La Jeune Parque* had served as a derivative; in 1940 he composed his IIIe Faust—he wrote to Vallery-Radot: "I have worked enormously as a derivative, without which I think I would have died of rage and despair." (*Œuvres*, I, p. 67.) *Mon Faust*, which, as far as I know, has little or no definite relation to the notes in the *cahiers*, consists of two unfinished dramatic works, *Lust, la demoiselle de cristal*, "comédie," —of which three acts out of four were written—, and *Le Solitaire ou les malédictions d'univers*, "féerie dramatique," of which, according to the author's prefatory note, only two thirds had been completed.[13]

Of these two unfinished plays, the comedy, *Lust*, is the more interesting. Lust is the charming young secretary of the aged and illustrious Faust. The other characters are Mephistopheles and his three demon-slaves, Belial, Astoroth and Goungoune, the incubus-succubus, and a young disciple, who comes to sit at the feet of the master, but who is rebuffed by the austere superiority of Faust. There is a suggestion that Mephistopheles has lost his power over men; he admits that Faust is too complicated for him to understand, and when he tempts the disciple, the young man is indifferent to the temptations. The disciple falls in love with Lust, who herself is in love with Faust. The play seems to me loosely constructed: in the first act, Faust indicates that he needs the help of Mephistopheles in writing a great work he plans. But this project is not alluded to in the remaining acts. The absence of the fourth and concluding act may indicate that Valéry did not know how to end his play. The fragments published in *Paul Valéry vivant* (see note 13) suggest that the fourth act would have been primarily concerned with the situation between Faust and his secretary, Lust.

The interest of this comedy is maintained by the dialogues. The interchanges between Faust and Lust, Faust and Mephistopheles, Mephistopheles and the disciple oscillate between paradox and profundity, and the wit is constant. In *Lust,* Valéry returned to the tone of ironic humor that, more than twenty years earlier, he had used so successfully in the poem, "Ebauche d'un serpent."

Le Solitaire seems to me less successful, principally because its state of incompleteness prevents us from understanding exactly what Valéry was trying to say in this "dramatic fairytale." The last scene is an *intermède,* in which Faust, fallen into some sort of abyss, carries on, with two sprites, a dialogue in alexandrines that remind one somewhat of the verses of the "Fragments du Narcisse." At sixty-nine, the author of *Charmes* was still a very competent versifier.

We cannot classify the lectures on poetry and poetics, given regularly at the Collège de France from December, 1937, until a few months before the poet's death in 1945, as among the major literary events of the poet's last years, since we have little basis on which to judge them. The introductory lecture is the only one published in the *Œuvres* (I, pp. 1340–1358). Notes from the lectures of the first years were printed in an obscure review, *Yggdrasill.*[14] If Jean Hytier, who found room for so many little-known texts of Valéry in the abundant notes of his Pléiade edition, did not include these notes, is it because he was uncertain as to how well they represented Valéry's lectures, or was it because to him, as to me, they are not very interesting? Possibly overaware of the seriousness of the situation, the author of *La Jeune Parque* seems to have become mired in abstract philosophi-

cal and psychological considerations without ever getting to the
real point. After listening to these lectures for several months,
I doubt if the faithful audience was much further advanced in its
knowledge of what poetry *is*. This is to be contrasted, incidentally, with the simplicity and the effectiveness of the essay of
1935, "Questions de poésie" (written as a preface for the *Anthologie des poètes de la N R F*), which, if it doesn't settle the almost impossibly difficult question of what poetry *is*, does handle
conclusively the question of what poetry *is not*. (*Œuvres*, I, pp.
1280–1294.)

The *Introduction biographique* to the *Œuvres* gives a detailed
account of Valéry's last years, the War years. It is not necessary
to repeat the details. He enjoyed the happiness of participating
—if from a distance—in the liberation of Paris. In spite of de-
clining health in the winter of 1945, he continued to give his
course. It was at the end of May that he was obliged to take to
his bed, and he died July 20, 1945. It is strange that the last
sentence (June or July, 1945) written by this unbeliever in his
last *cahier* reads as follows: "Le mot Amour ne s'est trouvé
associé au nom de Dieu que depuis le Christ." (The word Love
has been associated with the name of God only since Christ.)
(*Cahiers*, vol. 29, p. 911.)

The funeral of Paul Valéry was a national ceremony—held
between the two pavilions of the Palais de Chaillot, between his
four inscriptions. On July 27 he was buried in the *Cimetière
marin* of Sète; the fifth and sixth verses of the poem were en-
graved on his tomb: "O récompense après une pensée / Qu'un
long regard sur le calme de Dieux." (O recompense after a
thought / A long glance at the calm of the Gods.)

This unusual man, who at the age of twenty-one had said
"no" to a conventional literary career, who had said "no" (within
himself at least) to so many things in life, had now joined the
non-being (*non-être*) for which he had always felt a fascination.
One of his most significant statements (made by the serpent in
the "Ebauche d'un serpent" of 1921, but earlier by Valéry himself
—in a *cahier* of 1912) is that the "universe is merely a defect in
the purity of the non-being."

CHAPTER 5

The Poetic Theory of Paul Valéry

AFTER Jean Hytier, who in 1953 published a book of more than 300 pages on *La Poétique de Valéry*, one might be inclined to decide that there is nothing more to be said on the subject. But with the revelation to the public since then of thousands of pages of *cahiers*, in which Valéry expressed himself frequently—and at certain periods, almost constantly—on this subject (and this was a source not available to M. Hytier), there *is* something more to be said. In his *cahiers* Valéry developed and expatiated on certain phases of his poetic theory in a way not found in his published writings.

In any case, a book like the present one requires a briefer and simpler presentation than that found in M. Hytier's sizeable treatise. My own orientation of the problem will be somewhat different. I shall not, incidentally, make any effort to show a chronological evolution in the theories of the author of *La Jeune Parque;* these theories did not evolve; they became more and more detailed, more and more precise in the active poetic period of 1912–1922, then remained unchanged in later notes. I shall take up successively and as systematically as possible different aspects of Valéry's poetics, admitting that the divisions that I make are not always clearcut. Valéry's principal preoccupation in these matters recurs frequently—especially in the *cahiers*— and conforms to a certain pattern; so much so that when on occasion he starts out to write on one aspect of poetry, he will be found coming back to his basic concern: the effect of poetic composition *on the poet himself.*

I The Intent of the Poet

In other words, why did he write poetry? We know that with regard to literature in general Valéry's attitude was mainly negative, that he claimed that everything he had ever written was an *ouvrage de commande*,[1] and that, when, in 1919, the review of the young dadaists (Breton, Aragon, and Soupault), *Littérature*, hoping to get ridiculous answers, questioned a large number of writers: "Pourquoi écrivez-vous?" (why are you a writer?), in the December, 1919, number Valéry answered: "Par faiblesse" (through weakness). In a moment of annoyance, in 1922, he extended the same general attitude to poetry, exclaiming to André Gide: "It's by accident that I have written poetry." [2]

Somewhat more positive statements are to be found in the *cahiers:* here is a rather explicit one, written in 1917:

My intent was never to be a poet, nor to write verses as an action or as a principal function of my destiny. But I have at times chosen to act as if I was one and as good a one as possible, bringing to bear all the attention and all the powers of combination and analysis at my command, so as to penetrate into a poetic state at its purest, without remaining there: as a proof, as a means, as an exercise, as a sacrifice to certain divinities. (*Cahiers,* vol. 6, p. 568.)

Several years later (1923), he said:

A poet, a maker of verse, can propose for himself three objects; 1. produce such and such an impression on such and such readers; 2. obtain such and such effects and personal profit from his work (for his own interest); 3. obtain upon himself and for himself modifications caused by the essence of poetry. The three divisions are subdivided; every poet can be defined by the proportion of the three tendencies. (*Cahiers,* vol. 9, p. 632.)

In Valéry's case, his intention, in writing poetry, is, as we saw in the last quotation, inseparable from his constant preoccupation with the effect of the poet's labor upon the poet himself. This theory (that is, the theory of the importance of this effect), illustrations of which are very numerous, seems to me to belong in the section which I call "the philosophy of composition" (Chapter 5, part 4), and I shall present and discuss it there, also discussing the fact that Valéry's poems (maybe I should say his poetic projects) had often a genesis quite independent of any *intent* to write poetry.

II *What is Poetry?*

As I pointed out in the preceding chapter, in his published writings, such as the essay "Questions de poésie," Valéry was precise and clear in explaining what poetry *is not*. In his *cahiers*, including fragments collected in *Tel quel*, he made a number of efforts to define what poetry *is*. The following definition, one of the earliest I have found (in a *cahier* of 1914), is possibly too abstract to be enlightening:

Poetry is the art of causing (or simulating) accidental relations to be (or appear) regular, functional. Thus to present the accidents of coincidence of sounds and resonances, those of number—similitudes and images, etc.—as if they were the normal regimen (of a certain duration). And it is in that respect that poetry has so much relationship to memory in general, which makes of *past* incidents a regular functioning, a perpetual organ. (*Cahiers*, vol. 5, p. 151.)

In the fragments published in *Commerce* in 1929 under the title *Littérature*, we find a definition of poetry that will seem more meaningful to most readers:

Poetry is the effort to represent or to recreate, by means of articulate language, *those things* or *that thing* the expression of which is obscurely attempted by cries, tears, caresses, kisses, sighs, etc., and which *objects seem to wish to express* to the extent to which they have the appearance of life or of a supposed plan. . . .
Poetry is nothing but literature reduced to the essential of its active principle. It has been purged of *idols* of all kinds, of the illusions of realism and of the possible confusion between the language of "truth" and the language of "creation." (*Œuvres*, II, pp. 547–548.)

Another definition, in some respects the best of these, is to be found in notes for a lecture on "La Poésie pure" (1928):

Each time language manifests a *certain separation* from the most direct, that is, the least sensed expression of thought, each time these separations cause one to be aware, in some way, of a world of relationships distinct from the purely practical world, we conceive more or less clearly the possibility of enlarging this different domain, and we have the feeling that we are seizing the fragments of a noble and living substance which is perhaps susceptible of development and cultivation; and which, developed and utilized, constitutes poetry to the extent that poetry is an effect of artistic skill. (*Œuvres*, I, p. 1457.)

It is obvious that definitions of this sort apply only to the conception of poetry that has prevailed since Mallarmé (or since Baudelaire). Jean-Paul Sartre pointed out cogently in *Qu'est-ce que la littérature?*, after making a distinction between poetry and prose which Valéry would have accepted,[3] "that it is contemporary poetry that I am discussing. History shows us other forms of poetry." [4] Valéry himself, in his "Questions de poésie," called attention to the inadequacy for us today of former definitions of poetry, for instance, that of D'Alembert (1760)—" 'Here is the rigorous but just law which our century imposes on poets: it recognizes as good in verse only that which it would find excellent in prose'—which for us is a perfect definition of what poetry *is not*." (See *Œuvres*, I, p. 1292.) The type of poetry that Valéry wrote and attempted to define, while realizing, as Thierry Maulnier said in 1939,[5] that it is fundamentally undefinable, is frequently called "pure poetry" ("la poésie pure"). Did Valéry invent the term? He claimed to have. In a *cahier* of late 1926 or early 1927, he exclaims: "Pure poetry! I started the expression going . . ." (*Cahiers*, vol. 11, p. 877.) And he was certainly one of the first, if not the first, to use it: the first time in a published work was apparently in "Avant-propos à la 'Connaissance de la déesse'" in 1920 (*Œuvres*, I, p. 1275). In his *cahiers* he used the expression as early as 1911, in contrasting poetry and the novel, and he discussed the concept in detail later (see *Cahiers*, vol. 4, p. 488, and vol. 6, pp. 249 and 350—the later notes are 1916). The term was popularized in 1925, when Abbe Bremond discussed "pure poetry" (for him, Valéry wrote this kind of poetry) before the Academy, and a controversy ensued. Valéry's own conception of pure poetry was a severe one. No poems, including of course his own, were completely pure: "What one calls a poem is composed, in reality, of fragments of *pure poetry* encased in the matter of a discourse." (*Œuvres*, I, p. 1457.)

As I have suggested several times, it is easier to define poetry negatively than positively. For instance, Valéry found a certain type of harmony in poetry "undefinable."

The power of poetry resides in an *undefinable* harmony between what it *says* and what it *is*. "Undefinable" enters into the definition. This harmony must not be definable. When it is, it becomes *imitative* harmony, and that's not good. The impossibility of defining the relationship combined with the impossibility of defining its existence constitutes the essence of poetry. (*Cahiers*, vol. 7, p. 151—1918.)

Valéry's remarks, quoted earlier (page 73), on the meaning of the "Cimetière marin" are appropriate here. "The more a poem is in conformity to poetry, the less is it possible that it be thought in prose without perishing." (*Œuvres*, I, p. 1503.) This statement was made in 1933, but it represented a permanent opinion of Valéry, one that he expressed in a variety of ways over the years. Thus, in a *cahier* of 1906: "The beauty of verses and their power is that they cannot be thought . . ." (*Cahiers*, vol. 3, p. 858.) Twelve years later he said, more precisely: "You cannot put into prose what is really verse. The poem thus treated is denatured and loses everything. The less it loses in such an operation, the less it was worth before." (*Cahiers*, vol. 7, p. 123—see also p. 25.) And, in *Littérature* (1929), he quotes, with scorn, Boileau's line: "And my verse, good or bad, *always* says something." "There is the principle and the germ of an infinity of horrors." (*Œuvres*, II, p. 556.) Also, in *Rhumbs* (1927):

A poem of long duration is a poem of which one can make a *resumé*. But a *poem* is something of which you cannot make a *resumé*. You cannot make a resumé of a melody. You cannot make a resumé of anything beautiful. (*Œuvres*, II, p. 638.)

Finally, I shall quote an eloquent statement by our poet on the kind of poetry he did not want to write:

If poetry has to include silliness, if it has to be measured according to the capacity of inferior minds, if Musset is enough to satisfy you, if poetry is allowed to use crude methods, if a mosaic of images is a poem, then to hell with poetry. (*Cahiers*, vol. 9, p. 591—November, 1923.)

III *Form and Content*

Paul Valéry constantly insisted upon the basic validity of the paradoxical theory, which for him was not a paradox, that in poetry the form is more important than the content (or the subject) and should dominate it. In fact the content is often the product of the form, which precedes it. A few quotations, statements made at various periods, will illustrate this theory. A particularly eloquent version is this lapidary sentence, published in 1930, in *Choses tues*, but possibly written considerably earlier: "Beautiful works are daughters of their form, which is born before they are." (*Œuvres*, II, p. 477.) When one understands the difficulty that the creation of a beautiful form involves, one understands its superiority to the content:

If one were to represent to himself all the complicated activities that the creation or the adoption of a *form* presupposes, one would never stupidly put it in opposition to the *content*. . . . One is led to the *Form* by the concern of requiring the least possible contribution on the part of the reader—and even by leaving to oneself the least possible uncertainty and arbitrariness. (*Œuvres*, II, p. 554—*Littérature*, 1929.)

The *content* of a poem is closely related to the notion of the *subject*. Valéry made some striking remarks on the relative unimportance of the *subject* of a poem: "The *subject* of a poem is as foreign to it and as important to it as a man's *name* is to a man." (*Œuvres*, II, p. 679—*Autres Rhumbs*, 1927.) "The subject of a work is that to which a bad work is reduced." (*ibid.*)

The potential conflict between form and content in a poem often becomes a conflict between *sound* and *sense*. Valéry resumed this problem excellently in the following definition: "The poem, that prolonged hesitation between the sound and the sense." (*Cahiers*, vol. 4, p. 782—1913.) Twelve years later he discussed in some detail the question of this possible conflict:

Poetry. It is a very remarkable prejudice to think that the *sense* of the discourse is more exalted in dignity than the *sound* and the *rhythm*. If you understand poetry, you have surmounted this prejudice, which must not be very old, which is attached to the opposition, naïve and not immemorial, between the soul and the body, and to the exaltation of "thought," even when it is silly, at the expense of the existence and the actions of the body, even when these are admirable in exactness and elegance. (*Cahiers*, vol. 11, p. 230—1925.)

But the conflict exists: witness this brief complaint of the poet: "The poet says to himself—he is obliged to—'What a pity that this word, so *vocal*, doesn't have the meaning that I need.'" (*Cahiers*, vol. 3, p. 657—1905.) A vivid expression of the importance of *form* in any work of literature is this remark in *Autres Rhumbs* (1927): "The form is the skeleton of literary works; there are some which do not have any. All literary works die, but those which have a skeleton last much longer . . ." (*Œuvres*, II, p. 679.)

And in poetry Valéry insisted not only upon the necessity of form, but also that the form be rigorous; that the existing rules for regular French verse be observed completely. This belief is expressed definitively in a well-known passage in "Au sujet d'Adonis":

I cannot keep myself from being intrigued by the sort of obstinacy with which poets of all periods—up to the days of my youth—loaded themselves down with voluntary chains. . . . To write regular verses is undoubtedly to submit oneself to a law strange, rather senseless, always difficult, sometimes atrocious; it removes from existence an infinity of beautiful possibilities; it summons from far off a multitude of thoughts which did not expect to be conceived. . . . All the innumerable beauties which will be left in the mind, all those which the obligation of riming, which rhythm, which the incomprehensible rule of hiatus prevent from coming to life, all this seems to us to constitute an immense loss which one can truly lament. Let us however try to find a matter for rejoicing in this. . . . The requirements of a strict prosody are the artifice which confers upon natural language the qualities of a resistant matter. . . ." (*Œuvres*, I, pp. 477, 478, 480.) [6]

IV *The Philosophy of Composition*

I have given a somewhat pretentious title to this section, since I am unable to find a satisfactory English translation for the French "le travail du poète"—which is what the chapter is really about. I have borrowed from Poe, who gave this same pretentious title to his rather spurious account of the composition of "The Raven." Valéry, who (like Mallarmé) took Poe's "Philosophy of Composition" more seriously than was warranted, would not have objected to certain aspects of the poet's activity being thus categorized.

The first point to be considered is the concept (peculiar to Valéry, I believe) of the poem as primarily an *exercise*. A note in a *cahier* of 1923, referring surely to *Charmes*, says: "It is a strange feeling to see in a collection those poems which I wrote at quite different and quite distant periods and under diverse impressions but always in the same spirit—as exercises." (*Cahiers*, vol. 9, p. 526.) Much earlier (1905) he had expressed a very similar opinion: "Poetry has never been an objective for me, but an instrument, an exercise . . ." (*Cahiers*, vol. 3, p. 610.)

But if poetry was for Valéry an "exercise," what was the justification for indulging in it? The corollary was that the most important factor in poetic composition was the effect upon the poet of this activity. In 1913 he wrote in his *cahiers:*

The reaction of the labor of the mind upon the mind itself is so important that very often it deserves to be considered longer, more attentively than the labor or the product of that labor. The benefaction . . . or the malefaction of this reaction is very frequently more important than the literary work itself. The byproduct is thus more important than the product. The effort expended by the poet and the poem interest me less than the subtleties and the enlightenment acquired during the effort. And that is why one must labor over oneself. The poem will be for the others, that is, for the superficial quality, the initial shock, the effect, the expenditure, while the effort will be for myself—that is, for the duration, the continuation, the profit, the progress. . . . (*Cahiers*, vol. 5, p. 25.)

Nine years later he wrote a long note in which he explained more explicitly this theory, which he considered revolutionary:

Revolution. It was a revolution, an immense change, which was the basis of my story. It is to situate the artistic effort which one puts into the literary work in the construction of the work. To consider the composing itself as the principal thing, or to treat it as if it were the literary work, as if it were a dance, a construction of acts and expectations. Writing a poem is a poem. Solving a problem is a game with rules; chance, uncertainty are definite elements of the game. The impotence of the mind, its hesitations, its anguish are not surprises—or indefinite losses. But the *act of creation* is the principal thing, and some object or other which is created is an accessory: that is my idea.

It is not worth the trouble to write if it is not for the purpose of reaching the summit of one's being. . . . (*Cahiers*, vol. 8, p. 578.)

This long development is effectively epitomized in a sentence found in a *cahier* of 1925: "The essential object for me is not the literary work (a misunderstanding), it is the education of the author." (*Cahiers*, vol. 11, p. 126.) And what is the result? In *Autres Rhumbs* (1927) he defines it this way: "The literary work modifies the author; with each of the movements it draws out of him he undergoes an alteration. When finished, it reacts once more upon him." (*Œuvres*, II, p. 673.)

Before examining in some detail Paul Valéry's more specific ideas regarding the technique of poetic composition, it seems advisable to me to consider his attitude toward an element often held to be a major factor in the production of a poem: I am speaking of *inspiration*. Is there such a thing? Is it an important element of poetic composition? Our poet's attitude here may seem somewhat ambiguous, but if we examine it carefully, we will find that the ambiguity is superficial. To resume Valéry's position, he felt—and said so on numerous occasions—that the notion that a poem can be "dictated" to a poet by inspiration *alone* is ridiculous, but that nevertheless inspiration does play a rôle in poetic composition.

The following are typical expressions of his hostility to inspiration; the first undated (published in *Rhumbs*, 1926), the second in a *cahier* of 1921, the third in a *cahier* of 1924:

Inspiration. Supposing that inspiration is what people think it is—which is absurd, and which implies that a *whole poem* can be dictated to its author by some deity—this would result rather precisely in the fact that an inspired person could write just as well in a language other than his own and which he did not know.

The inspired person could similarly be unfamiliar with his period, the conditions of taste in his period, the works of his predecessors and his rivals—unless you make inspiration into a power so refined, so articulate, so sagacious, so well informed and so calculating that you might as well call it Intelligence and Knowledge. (*Œuvres*, II, p. 628.)

It is an unbearable image for poets which represents them receiving from imaginary creatures the best part of their works. Agents of transmission—that's a concept of savages. As for me I want none of it. I make use only of that chance which is at the basis of all minds, and add to it stubborn labor, which is opposed to that chance. (*Cahiers*, vol. 8, p. 275.)

Suppose that some poem perfectly beautiful should come to you in a dream. Will you dare to claim it as yours? Under what name will you publish it? What is the name of this author? Why wouldn't it be yours? If it was a crime, you would reject it. One doesn't sin by a dream? And yet . . . Inspiration is then irresponsibility. (*Cahiers*, vol. 10, p. 247.)

In the preceding quotations, the terms, "a whole poem," "the best part of their works," "a perfectly beautiful poem," are the key words. Valéry was condemning the notion that inspiration *alone* is sufficient for the poet. In a passage often quoted, he expresses a similar opinion with regard to the kindred notion of *enthusiasm*. "I found unworthy and still do writing on the basis of enthusiasm alone. Enthusiasm is not a mood for the writer." ("Note et digression," 1919—*Œuvres*, I, p. 1205.) Valéry's idea of the *real* rôle of inspiration in the technique of poetic composition is revealed in his theory of *vers donnés* or *trouvés* ("given" or "found" verses) opposed to *vers faits* or *calculés* ("made" or "calculated" verses).

This theory might be said to have a basis in a mention of the positive aspect of the poet's inspiration—and its limitation:

The Pythoness would not be able to dictate a poem. But a verse—that is, one unit—and then another. This goddess of the Continuum is incapable of continuing. It is the Discontinuum that fills the gaps. (*Cahiers*, vol. 4, p. 808—1912—printed in *Rhumbs*, *Œuvres*, II, p. 628.)

Five years earlier he discussed in detail how a long poem may have its origin in a single verse which "comes" to the poet:

In a number of cases, a poet writes a long poem by means of and because of a single *verse* which came to him first of all, and seemed good to him (that is, *independent, autonomous, found,* acquired definitively and representing perfection). This verse came to him by a state rather similar to dream, a state complete and well isolated, partial: the state of perfect functioning of a partial system, auditive or other. . . .

It is a question of making with this verse a poem. Then the novel (*sic*) begins to become prolonged, become coordinated, etc., and the difficulty consists in placing oneself in states *worthy* of the first verse. The devilishly hard thing is to continue. (*Cahiers*, vol. 4, p. 162—1908.)

Two passages collected in *Tel quel,* 1, discuss the problem of *vers trouvés* and *vers faits* (or *calculés*). Both of these deserve to be quoted. One comes from *Cahier B 1910,* a portion of the *cahiers* reproduced photographically in 1924—the first selection from the *cahiers* to be revealed to the public:

There are verses that one *finds.* The others, one *makes* them. One perfects those that have been *found.* One "naturalizes" the others. A double simulation in a contrary direction to attain that falsity: perfection . . . equally distant from pure spontaneity, which is no matter what, and from productions completely directed by the will, which are painful, tenuous, capable of being denied by any other will, incapable of subduing someone else. (*Œuvres,* II, p. 591.)

I shall quote the other passage from a *cahier* of 1919 (in the published version Valéry added an over-subtle final paragraph that is confusing):

Two sorts of verses: the given verses (and which are given generally as if by music) and the *calculated* verses. The calculated verses are those which are presented necessarily under the form of problems to be solved—and which have for initial conditions the *given* verses, and then rime, syntax, the meaning already involved in the given verse. (*Cahiers,* vol. 7, p. 388.)

The part played by rime in this theory is worth noting. For Valéry, rime here is not a constraint but a guide: an attitude to be contrasted with that of Voltaire, who said, two centuries earlier: "The first verse is for the sense, the second for the rime." [7] Valéry no doubt was unfamiliar with this statement; if he had been I think he would have commented on it. It is in notes of 1920 that we find rather precise remarks on the rôle of rime in helping one to obtain the necessary "calculated" verses. First this:

The good God gives us the first verse free, but it's up to us to make the second, which must rime with the other and not be unworthy of its supernatural brother. All the resources of the mind and of one's experience are not superfluous when it comes to making a verse sufficiently similar to the one which was a gift. (*Cahiers,* vol. 7, p. 483.)

Then, some months later:

In a distich the first verse that of chance, happy and immediate: *ex nihilo*. The second is that of the intellect imitating chance and God. . . . Rime is a marvelous regulator of intellectual functions. It obliges one to will, after having undergone, to meditate, after having received. In a quatrain with crossed rimes, AB is luck, CD labor. But A and C must *a priori* have the relation of ending with the same syllable, and B and D similarly. Therefore a reduction of possibilities. (*Cahiers*, vol. 7, p. 730.)

It is thus quite evident that Valéry was in complete opposition to Boileau on the subject of rime, and said so quite explicitly: "Reason requires that the poet prefer rime to reason." (*Œuvres*, II, p. 676—*Autres Rhumbs*, 1927.) He gleefully pointed out:

Rime has this great success of infuriating stupid people who think naïvely that there is something more important than a convention. They have the naïve belief that some thought *can* be more profound, more durable . . . than any convention whatever . . . . That is not the least of rime's charms, and on account of which it caresses the ear no less sweetly. (*Œuvres*, II, p. 551.) [8]

To turn from the abstract to the concrete, Valéry illustrated his theory of "given" verses and "calculated" verses, the latter helped into being by rime, with a reference to a famous poem by Baudelaire:

La Servante au Grand Cœur (the great-hearted servant). This celebrated verse[9] which contains a whole Balzac novel in its twelve syllables—people have gone so far as to explain it by a story of a servant. The truth is simpler. It is evident to a poet—the fact is that the verse *came* to Baudelaire and that it was born with its air of a sentimental ballad, of a silly and touching reproach. And Baudelaire continues. He buried the cook in a lawn (*pelouse* in French, which rimes richly with *jalouse*), which is not according to custom but according to the rime. (*Œuvres*, II, p. 556—this quotation and the previous one are from *Littérature*, 1929.)

Earlier in this book I mentioned two verses of Valéry, which, according to his own statements were "donnés": the first verse of "La Fileuse," "Assise la fileuse au bleu de la croisée," and the fifth verse of "La Pythie," "Pâle, profondément mordue."

After the theory of "found" or "given" verses and "calculated" verses, which is the basis of Valéry's concept of poetic composition, I shall note other details. He is constantly antirationalistic. The poet makes use of ideas, but only in a limited way, as the following statements show:

"The idea" for a poet is not much more than a rudder. It guides, but is flexible. In vain you wish to mount against the wind. In vain you wish to go to some particular point. Let it be sufficient for you to wish to go somewhere. Take what the wind brings. (*Œuvres*, II, p. 551—*Littérature*, 1929.)

Verses. The vague idea, the intention, the varied and imaged impulsion being broken by the regular forms, the invisible defenses of conventional prosody: this engenders new things and unforeseen figures. There are astonishing consequences of this shock of the will and the feelings against the insensibility of conventions. (*Œuvres*, II, p. 551—*Littérature*, 1929.)

Thus, in taking as point of departure a "given" verse, and guided by the necessity of finding rimes, and, in many poems, of constructing a stanza with a fixed form, the poet at times comes upon a "heureux hasard" (a stroke of luck) or a "heureux accident" (a lucky accident), a "trouvaille" (a discovery), or even occasionally what Valéry, using a Latin term, calls a *felix culpa* (a lucky mistake):

Poetry proceeds from an initial stroke of luck, but one verse is not a poem, nor a subject, nor an impression. Then one must produce a rather large number of secondary strokes of luck so that the whole may give the impression of the exceptional become obedient, of the most improbable become the easiest. (*Cahiers*, vol. 5, p. 152—1914.)

One must profit by the lucky accident. The true writer abandons his idea for the benefit of another which appears before him while he is seeking words for the required idea, and it appears in these words themselves. He finds himself having become more powerful, even more profound, by this unforeseen word game. (*Œuvres*, II, p. 577—*Cahier B 1910.*)

The theory of the positive value of the *lapsus*, of the *felix culpa* is not surprisingly one of Valéry's "bad" thoughts: "*Lapsus*, admirable thing, dispenses sometimes some very happy mistake,

felix culpa: it was a good slip of the tongue." (*Œuvres,* II, p. 908
—*Mauvaises pensées et autres,* 1941.) But the "Doctor" had
already said more or less the same thing in the dialogue, *L'Idée
fixe:*

The same mental event which, psychologically, is or should be assimi-
lated to a waste product, which is caused by fatigue, or local exhaus-
tion, or a bit of chance, a local reaction comparable to a *lapsus linguæ,*
can, in another situation, take on a literary value. . . . It can give a
very successful little effect, very new, which the consciousness appre-
ciates, receives, notes. . . . (*Œuvres,* II, p. 222.)

In his notes on poetic composition, Paul Valéry keeps returning to the anti-rationalistic opinion that it is in the arbitrary labor
of constructing a poem in a fixed form, according to the most
rigorous rules of classical French prosody, that one often comes
upon the most charming ideas or images:

A charming, touching, "profoundly human" idea comes sometimes
from the need of uniting two stanzas, two developments. It was necessary to bridge a gap, or weave threads which would make certain the
continuation of the poem, and, as the always possible continuation is
man himself or a man's life, this formal need finds a reply; arbitrary
in the case of the author. . . . (*Cahiers,* vol. 7, p. 161—1918 or 1919.)

An integral part of the theory of poetic composition is the idea
of the importance of *corrections,* "ce tripotage" (fiddling around)
as Valéry calls it:

The accustomed labor of verses, this fiddling around which leads to
perfection, brings one to become accustomed to changes of words, to
suppressions, to substitutions, which, by their rather frequent satisfy-
ing success, displace the point of view of the writer, and cause him
legitimately to think that the initial object and the primitive plan of
his poem are not essential; that one can and must abandon them, if a
stroke of luck which moves away from them presents itself. . . . In
other words he understands that it is the end which is attained by the
means and not by the inarticulate desire and the primitive occasion
or the emotion. (*Cahiers,* vol. 9, p. 647—1923.)

The correction itself can come as a stroke of luck ("heureux
hasard"):

A successful correction, an impromptu solution, can declare itself as a result of a sudden glance at the page which you had abandoned because it had displeased you. Everything wakes up. You had started out wrong. Everything becomes verdant. The new solution brings out an important word, frees it—just as in chess a play frees this bishop or that pawn who is going to be able to act. Without this play the work did not exist. With this play it exists immediately. (*Œuvres*, II, pp. 552–553, *Littérature*, 1929,—taken with slight modifications from *Cahiers*, vol. 6, pp. 204–205—1916.)

As we have seen, Valéry preferred to work in fixed forms, and, as a form, he seems to have preferred above all the sonnet. He wrote many sonnets, and praised the sonnet as a form a number of times. Most eloquent of his remarks in praise of the sonnet is a passage in the article "De la Diction des vers" (1926), in which he imagines a meeting in the underworld with the inventor of the sonnet. He addresses him thus:

My dear colleague, I greet you very humbly. I don't know how good your poems are; I haven't read them, and I wager that they are no good, because it is always safe to bet that poems are no good; but no matter how bad they may be—flat, insipid, clear, silly, naïvely fabricated—still I place you in my heart above all poets of the earth and the underworld! You invented a *form*, and the greatest of poets adapted themselves to this form. (*Œuvres*, II, p. 1254.)

Some year earlier, in a *cahier* of 1922, he had in a similar vein proclaimed: "Glory to the inventor of the sonnet." This note explained Valéry's conception of the perfect sonnet, in which "each of the four parts would perform a function different from that of the others, and these differences would be justified by the *life* of the whole discourse." (*Cahiers*, vol. 8, p. 774.) In a note written some months earlier he had made an attempt (which didn't make much sense to this particular reader) to reduce a sonnet to algebraic formulas, after which came some curious remarks on the function of the rimes of a sonnet:

The same rimes in the quatrains have a meaning that must be found. *Writing the sonnet is finding that meaning.* It is finding one of the expressions or solutions of this relationship: *the same rimes.* (A good sonnet would make one feel that the two quatrains *had to* rime with each other.) (*Cahiers*, vol. 8, p. 357.)

An unusual element in Valéry's philosophy of composition is his theory of variants or "multiple solutions." He made this theory public in a few lines of "Au sujet du 'Cimetière marin.'"

I have been blamed, for example, for having given several texts, even contradictory ones, of the same poem. This reproach does not seem to me very intelligible. . . . On the contrary, I should be tempted, if I followed my feeling in this matter, to engage poets to produce, in a way similar to musicians, a diversity of variants or solutions of the same subject. Nothing would seem to me more in conformity to the idea that I like to entertain of a poet and of poetry. (*Œuvres*, I, p. 1501—1933.)

He had expressed this idea before, as early as 1903, in a striking image: "The vine and the fig tree are two solutions of the same problem." (*Cahiers*, vol. 3, p. 103.) And, in 1922, in somewhat the same terms as in 1933: "A poem with variants is a scandal for the ordinary and vulgar opinion. For me it's a merit. The intelligence is defined by the number of variants." (*Cahiers*, vol. 9, p. 49.)

Finally he put the theory into practice by publishing, in 1926, the sonnet "Féerie (variante)"; and in the subsequent editions of the *Album de vers anciens* he put "Féerie" and "Même Féerie" on facing pages.[10]

The last element in Valéry's philosophy of composition to be discussed in this chapter—that of "non-finishing"—rejoins to some extent the earlier theme of the importance of the effect of his poetic labors on the poet himself. We saw earlier, in connection with the "Cimetière marin" (pages 74–75), that Valéry claimed that this particular poem was published before it was finished. This fits in with Valéry's theory that a poem is *never* really *finished*. Thus, in *Littérature* (1929):

A poem is never finished—it is always an accident that terminates it, that is, gives it to the public. This is caused by weariness, by the demand of the publisher, by the thrust of another poem. But never does the condition of the work (if the author is not a fool) show that it could not be pushed, changed, considered as a first approximation or the origin of a new investigation. I conceive, as for myself, that the same subject and almost the same words could be reprised indefinitely and occupy a whole life. "Perfection" is labor. (*Œuvres*, II, p. 553.)

Let us remember that, for Valéry, his objective was not the literary work itself. This long statement to that effect will make a fitting conclusion to our study of his philosophy of composition:

For most men, to create a work is a problem which is solved when the work itself is created. The work is the objective which absorbs, absolves, consumes the means.

But for me it is otherwise. My invincible opinion causes me to consider the work as a stage of a development of which the means are a part. My objective is not the work, but the creating of the work by the means, and these means subjected to the conditions of sharpness, clarity, elegance which one expects in general from the work and not from its elaboration. To build to the sound of the lyre. The profound meaning that could be given to that fable. (*Cahiers,* vol. 9, p. 655—1923.) [11]

CHAPTER 6

Paul Valéry's Rank and Lasting
Importance as a Poet

FOUR years after Paul Valéry's death, the weekly, *Les Nouvelles littéraires*, published, December 29, 1949, the results of an investigation: to designate by vote the ten persons who were the most celebrated, the most important, the most representative of the half century which was just ending. Paul Valéry was ranked sixth, behind Einstein, Bergson, Proust, Debussy and Gide. He received the same number of votes as his friend Louis de Broglie and ranked ahead of Freud, Picasso and Claudel.

Would Valéry hold that rank today? It is hard to say. Let us recall his own statement: "Great men die twice, once as men, once as great men." (*Œuvres*, II, p. 592—*Cahier B 1910*.) But Valéry's position as a "great" man is not the subject of this chapter; I shall leave that for history to decide. It is with his position as a poet that I am concerned here.

How can a man be ranked as a great poet, or as a poet at all, when he says "I don't give a damn for poetry" (mais je m'en fous, moi, de la poésie)?[1] This was his irritated reaction when he was spoken of as the great poet of the twentieth century. But we saw in the preceding chapter, where I quoted so liberally from the *Cahiers*, that Valéry was constantly preoccupied with the problems confronting the poet, and we also know that at certain periods of his life he devoted much time and great efforts to poetic composition. His "I don't give a damn for poetry" applies to much of the poetry of his time, to many of the poets, and above all to his own *public* recognition as a great poet, but there is abundant evident to show that he had a very high regard for poetry of real quality, for what he called "pure" or "absolute" poetry.

Some admirers of Paul Valéry—apparently considering that this was a way to confirm his rank as a major poet—have attempted to find a unity in his work, especially in the volume,

Charmes. As early as 1927, Emilie Noulet (*Paul Valéry*, Bruxelles, 1927) advanced the thesis that *Charmes* has a "subject" and that this subject, the drama of intellectual or artistic creation, is expressed symbolically, in one way or another, in each of the poems of *Charmes.* As partial substantiation of this thesis, Madame Noulet claimed that the order in which the poems appeared was planned in view of this "subject." Daniel Gallois, in *L'Information littéraire* of May, 1956, and J. R. Lawler, in *Lecture de Valéry* (Paris, 1964), have in general accepted this thesis. Jacques Duchesne-Guillemin (*Etude de Charmes*, Bruxelles, 1947) and Pierre-Olivier Walzer (*La Poésie de Valéry*, Genève, 1953) presented a strong objection to Madame Noulet's "substantiation" in pointing out that the order of poems upon which her argument was based did not exist in the first edition of *Charmes*, where the arrangement, with one or two exceptions, was alphabetical. A reader of *Charmes* who is not desirous of proving a thesis will note that the definitive arrangement of the poems was in fact not haphazard or arbitrary, but seemed aimed at producing harmonious contrasts between poems of differing forms, lengths, and subjects.

The best refutation of the thesis of unity and a "subject" in *Charmes* are statements made by the poet himself, statements which we have no reason to doubt. A remark cited earlier applies equally well here: "It is a strange feeling to see in a *collection* those poems which I wrote at quite different and quite distant periods and under *diverse* impressions, but always in the same spirit—as exercises." (*Cahiers*, vol. 9, p. 526, 1923. The italics in this quotation were mine.) Thus the only unity that Valéry saw in *Charmes* was that the poems were all what he called "exercises." A typical reaction of the poet to symbolic interpretations of certain of his poems is this note in one of his later *cahiers*: "*Les Pas*: a little poem purely sentimental, to which people attach an intellectual meaning, calling it a symbol of 'inspiration!'" (*Cahiers*, vol. 28, p. 427.)

I am not trying to assert that *none* of Valéry's poems has a possible symbolic interpretation or to claim that he never treated in his poetry the subject of artistic creation. Several poems of *Charmes*, to wit "Aurore," "La Pythie," "Poésie," "Ode secrète," are variations on this subject. Others, such as "Fragments du Narcisse," "Ebauche d'un serpent," and "Le Cimetière marin," have quite different subjects, and, furthermore, it is ill-advised to attempt, as has been done, to find symbolic interpretations for poems that are, to use the poet's own term, "purely sentimental," such as "Les Pas" (mentioned above), "La Dormeuse" or "La Fausse morte." And delicate impressions such as "La Ceinture," "Le Sylphe," and "L'Insinuant," are not benefited by weighty interpretations.

What is or what will be Valéry's final place in French poetry? Is he the last of a line, a relatively short line, proceeding from Baudelaire (and Poe) through Mallarmé? French poetry since Max Jacob, born in 1876, and Guillaume Apollinaire, born in 1880, five and nine years after Valéry, respectively, can be said to have followed, more or less, the other line, descended from Baudelaire also, but turned in another direction by Rimbaud. Is Valéry the last important French poet to have observed meticulously the classical rules of French prosody? Possibly. He himself said: "Poetry is a survival." (*Œuvres,* II, p. 548—*Littérature,* 1929.)

By 1925, at least, the young poets of the dadaist-surrealist group, who at first published his poems in their review,[2] and, as late as 1921, admired him (with a few exceptions),[3] undoubtedly considered Valéry himself as nothing more than a survivor of an outdated type of poetry. The surrealists' "automatic" writing was probably not completely automatic—it is certain, moreover, that the poetry of Paul Eluard, the best of the surrealist poets, contains a large amount of conscious craftsmanship—but it is obvious that the significant French poetry written since 1925 is based upon an esthetic quite different from that of the author of the "Cimetière marin."

To place Valéry as a poet it is best to compare him to the other poets of his generation, the poets born between 1860 and 1880. Jules Laforgue, born in 1860, might have become a major poet if he had lived longer. The work that he had time to complete in the twenty-seven years of his life is that of a minor poet of distinction and unfulfilled promise. Guillaume Apollinaire should be rated as a major poet, but he is really of a later generation, as is Max Jacob also, in spite of the date of his birth. None of Jacob's significant poetry antedates 1900. The other contemporaries of Valéry, from Henri de Régnier, born in 1864, to Léon-Paul Fargue, born in 1878, including Francis Vielé-Griffin (1864),

Francis Jammes (1868), and Paul Fort (1872), wrote a substantial amount of agreeable minor poetry, almost all of it in their youth, before 1900. None of these poets, however, is of the stature of Paul Valéry, even of the Valéry of before 1900. Whereas it might be claimed that their best work is on the same level as "La Fileuse" (and some would dispute this), the "Narcisse parle" of the same date is already on a higher level, and the poems of the period known as the "majority": "Vue," "Eté," "Valvins" and "Profusion du soir," for example, rank well above anything of which Régnier, Vielé-Griffin, Jammes, Fort or Fargue was capable. And each of these poets said all he had to say in his youth; none of them had, like Valéry, a period of ripe, significantly productive maturity.

It is difficult to compare Valéry to two other writers of his generation, who are sometimes spoken of as major poets: Paul Claudel, born in 1868, and Charles Péguy, born in 1873. They are so very different. It seems certain that Claudel will go down to posterity as a major writer, and probably Péguy as well (though this is less certain), but was either of them really a major poet? Certainly not, according to Valéry's conception of poetry, and also certainly not, if one bases one's conception of poetry upon the practice of a whole line of the best modern French poets, running from Apollinaire through Saint-John Perse, Reverdy and Supervielle, and beyond them to Eluard and then to Michaux and Char. Paul Valéry is the best *poet* of a generation that included three other great writers, great in other domains: Paul Claudel, André Gide and Marcel Proust.

Will the future regard Paul Valéry as only a Malherbe, or even as only a Jean-Baptiste Rousseau, who, incidentally, as Valéry himself once said, was once a great poet and conceivably might someday become a great poet again?[4] At any rate, it is certain that he will not be judged to be the product of an artificially created vogue, as was suggested in 1931, in the *Journal littéraire* of Paul Léautaud, Valéry's probably jealous former friend: "I said to Madame Pascal that it seems as if they are about to play on us, with Fargue, the same trick they did with Valéry . . . She said to me: I think so. They are even mentioning him for the Academy, as they did with Valéry."[5]

In concluding, I note Berne-Joffroy's recent (1960) opinion as to the position of Paul Valéry as a poet:

As for the poems of Valéry, what will happen to them? He himself knew well that his art was inevitably something exceptional and risked ending up as a sort of laboratory product. . . . When *La Jeune Parque* appeared, many of the most refined and most enlightened connoisseurs of the period admired it immediately. Others had reservations; these reservations are more numerous today, at least in certain circles.[6] Perhaps the very studied quality of the poems of Valéry, which today can seem to be absence of poetry, will be precisely what will save them tomorrow. . . .

It is clear that neither Valéry nor his work corresponds to the idea that many of the best minds of today have of . . . a poet. . . .[7]

Let me say, as my final word on this, that I disagree with M. Berne-Joffroy, and that I consider Valéry to be a poet of the first rank. He does not, probably—and posterity will confirm or change this—belong at the summit, with Victor Hugo, Charles Baudelaire, Arthur Rimbaud and his own master, Stéphane Mallarmé, but a little below, on the same level as his until recently misjudged predecessor, Paul Verlaine.

CHAPTER 7

Valéry's Position as a Thinker

TO state Paul Valéry's position as a poet, which is a matter of opinion, based upon general impressions and feelings, rather than detailed analysis of subject-matter and ideas, required only a few pages. But to place him as a thinker and, incidentally as a prose writer (for it is in his prose that we find the primary expression of his thought), I feel it necessary to make a somewhat detailed analysis. This aspect was touched upon only briefly in preceding chapters.

I shall omit the writings on poetic theory, these having been accounted for in Chapter V. The writings in prose which I shall discuss can be classified as follows: 1. the notations of the Narcissistic thinker—the *cahiers* and the published works taken from them; 2. *Leonardo* and *Teste*—Valéry the antiphilosopher; 3. the Socratic dialogues—byplay of ideas—and *Mon Faust,* somewhat similar; 4. the literary criticism—or rather the ideas expressed by Valéry concerning literature and individual writers.

Two characteristics to be noted in all of Valéry's prose writings, even those that might be commissions of the most trifling or perfunctory nature (inscriptions for a public building or prefatory notice for an exposition), are the profundity, the originality of the thought and the perfection of the expression. Valéry was aware of his originality, which was the result of a conscious effort, characterized thus (in 1928):

Poe was the first to think of giving a pure theoretical basis to literary works. Mallarmé and myself. I think I was the first to try to avoid having any recourse at all to former notions—but to place everything upon a purely analytical basis. (*Cahiers,* vol. 12, p. 703.)

I *The Narcissistic Meditations*

Paul Valéry said several times that his only writings in prose were "sur demande ou commandés" (requested or commissioned).[1] He was not, however, in saying that, referring to what I am going to discuss in this section: his daily notes, the importance of which *for him* is obvious. It is not impossible that posterity will decide that these daily notes found in the twenty-nine volumes of the *Cahiers* (each containing some 900 pages) constitute one of the prose masterpieces of the Twentieth Century, and are Valéry's most important work. In their present form, the *Cahiers* are rather inaccessible to anyone but the specialist. In the first place, their bulk, their expense and the limited printing —1,100 copies—will keep them out of the library of the average reader of French literature (and, I fear, out of the average American college library). And their appearance (let me recall that the publication is a photograph of the texts): notes, formulas, equations, often very legible but occasionally almost illegible— for these were Valéry's personal notes, not destined for publication—all this is sufficient to frighten a novice. I well remember my own consternation the day in October, 1958, when I first opened the volume (volume 5 or volume 6, I am not sure which) that was placed before me on my table at the Bibliothèque Nationale.

I soon found, however, that ploughing through these volumes was fascinating, though immensely time-consuming. Since then, several studies of these *Cahiers* have been published. The late specialist on Valéry, Maurice Bémol, analyzed the early volumes in two articles in the *Revue d'Histoire littéraire de la France*.[2] After Bémol's death, J. R. Lawler made, in the same review, a similar study of later volumes.[3] A quite readable analysis of the work, volume by volume, has been made by Edmée de La Roche-foucauld in a series of articles appearing every few months in the *Revue de Paris*.[4] Finally, Judith Robinson, in her recent book, *L'Analyse de l'esprit dans les "Cahiers" de Valéry* (Paris, 1963), has discussed, and in my opinion justified, in more than 200 pages, her judgment that Valéry is "one of the modern thinkers who contributed the most to our knowledge of the mind and mental processes."[5]

Paul Valéry felt that these notes, jotted down, as I mentioned earlier, from day to day, were the expression of his most significant activity, and he said so on a number of occasions, indicating also under what conditions this activity took place. One of the most explicit of these statements is in the "Avant-propos" to *Analecta* (one of the publications of selections from his *cahiers* —1926):

For thirty years I have been keeping a record of my "essays" [he is using the term as Montaigne used it]. Hardly out of bed, before daybreak, between the lamp and the sunrise—a pure and profound hour— I have the custom of writing down that which invents itself in my mind. The idea of another person, a reader, is completely absent from these moments; in other words, the reader, that essential portion of a reasoned literary mechanism, is lacking. . . . These are then notes for myself only: impromptus, unexpected developments of my faculty of attention, embryoes; and not at all those elaborate productions, revised, consolidated, put into a calculated form, which can be presented to the whole public with the assurance and grace of works specially made for it. (*Œuvres*, II, pp. 700–701.)

Seventeen years later, in a letter to Father Rideau, who had just written an *Introduction à la pensée de Paul Valéry*, he represented these activities from a somewhat different angle:

It's been fifty or more years now that before dawn my head exercises me every day. This consists of two or three hours of interior maneuvering *that I need physiologically.* If this need is not satisfied, my whole day is affected: *I don't feel good.* I start to write what I have to give to the public only after this period which I grant myself or rather which I entrust to the hazards of the events of an awakening mind, a mind which on one day is more sensitive to one type of ideas and on another to another. . . . That is how I have lived from day to day. . . . My only constant preoccupation, my only permanent instinct has been probably to represent to myself more and more clearly my mental functioning. . . .
In a word, if one was willing to retain from out of my days only those few critical hours that I have mentioned, and annul or disregard the rest of my time, one would get a sort of *Monsieur Teste.* And if one was willing to examine the totality of the notes in my morning notebooks . . . one would easily find in these papers enough matter to construct an author having my name.[6]

These elaborate explanations give a rather definite idea of the importance that Paul Valéry attached to his *cahiers*. In a letter to André Gide, October, 1922, he epitomized it in these words: "Mon vrai moi est là" (my true self is there). (*Corresp. Gide-Valéry*, p. 493.) Before 1957–1961, when the *Cahiers* were published, this very important part of Valéry's work—and for him, as we have just seen, *this was* his work—was very little known. With one apparent exception, the *Cahier B 1910*, the extracts collected in the two volumes of *Tel quel* (plus those found in the *Mauvaises pensées et autres*), are merely selections of the most accessible portions of the notes, and do not give much idea of their real nature. And as to *Cahier B 1910*—I wonder. True, it is a faithful reproduction of pages 390–422 of volume 4 of the *Cahiers*. But, in the photographic reproduction, these pages are so legible, so comprehensible, so unabstruse, that I wonder if the author did not edit and recopy this portion of his notes specifically in view of the Edouard Champion photographic reproduction of 1924.

As the reader has already been able to observe, I made extensive use, in Chapter V of this book, of Valéry's jottings on poetic theory, as I discovered them in my reading of the *cahiers*, and I shall make similar use of the literary-critical notes in a later portion of this present chapter. For an analysis of the more abstruse portions of the *cahiers*, the profundities of Valéry's thought, I refer the reader to Judith Robinson's book, mentioned above.

In concluding this brief, maybe too brief, consideration of this most important section of Valéry's work, I must point out that the *cahiers* served as a reservoir of ideas for the poet. The ease with which he could treat a given subject which a publisher or an editor requested or commissioned is explained by the probability that he had already meditated extensively on that very subject, jotting down notes on it from time to time, and also surely retaining the fruits of these meditations in the vast reservoir of his brain. (Some sections of the *cahiers*, in the very active 1912–1920 period, contain indexes of subject-matter.) The published works, not only prose, but poetry as well (cf. my reference to the "Ebauche d'un serpent" at the end of Chapter IV) are thus merely—to use a respectable cliché—the exposed portion of the great iceberg of Paul Valéry's mental activity.

II *The Antiphilosopher*

Edmond Teste and Leonardo da Vinci are the embodiments or the projection, and in the latter case a rather abstract projection, of Valéry's intellectual ideal. I use the term "antiphilosopher" in the sense that Valéry was hostile to the "philosopher" as represented by those of the past—Plato or Descartes (that is, Descartes the metaphysician; Valéry admired Descartes as a man of science[7]) or Pascal or Kant—or, of the recent past, for example Bergson. He would have presumably considered such contemporary "philosophers" as Bertrand Russell or Wittgenstein as men of science or mathematicians rather than as philosophers.

The notion that Valéry was influenced by Bergson dies hard. Paul Valéry became acquainted with Henri Bergson in the twenties;[8] as fellow Academicians they had frequent contacts, and after Bergson's death in 1941, Valéry showed his courage and his independence by pronouncing before the Academy a eulogy of the dead philosopher. (*Œuvres*, I, pp. 883–886.) Praising a philosopher of the Jewish race was a sure way to win the disfavor of the German occupant. But he denied, as early as 1927, that the philosopher had any influence on him:

The influence of my illustrious and excellent colleague upon me never existed. It's a question of chronology and biography. My ideas took shape between 1892 and 1895. I mean my manner or method of judging. At that moment who knew Bergson? Moreover I have never studied philosophy, and I wouldn't dare to confess to you how deficient my culture is in that domain. . . .

Two or three years ago I read *L'Evolution créatrice*, and I admit to you that in spite of the great value of that work, it doesn't correspond at all to my own needs; a theory of the *élan vital* doesn't suit my type of mind. . . . Thibaudet was strangely mistaken with regard to me in that respect, and yet he knows me. I can't understand it. . . .[9]

Valéry stated on a number of occasions that he was *not* a philosopher: "the non-philosopher that I am" (1927—*Œuvres*, II, p. 1496); "all this is essentially anti-philosophical" (1933—*Œuvres*, II, p. 1498); "as for me, non-philosopher" (1943—*Œuvres*, II, p. 1504). Judith Robinson, with numerous quotations from the *cahiers* as her justification, pointed out in detail that

the basis of Valéry's quarrel with philosophy and philosophers
was in their misuse of language[10]—and in this he was in agreement with two philosophical schools of the present day: the
"analytical" philosophers of the English school and the "logical
positivists" of Vienna.

Edmond Teste and Leonardo da Vinci (Valéry's Leonardo
da Vinci, not necessarily the real one) represent therefore the
rigorous intellect which Valéry proposed as the ideal to replace
the philosopher. In Chapter II, I discussed in some detail the
figure of Monsieur Teste, a sort of monster carrying the principal
of intellectual rigor to the extreme. Valéry's Leonardo da Vinci
is more complicated, an attempt at a synthesis on which I shall
comment shortly. The abiding significance of Leonardo for
Valéry is shown by the fact that he kept returning to him.

As I explained earlier, the "Introduction à la méthode de
Léonard de Vinci" was an ouvrage de commande, and Valéry's
first such; it was written sometime between December, 1894,
and the early months of 1895. It was reprinted in 1919, with a
"Note et digression" added to it. In 1928, Valéry published in
Commerce an essay of some length, "Léonard et les philosophes."
When these three essays were reprinted in a volume entitled
Les divers Essais sur Léonard de Vinci de Paul Valéry, commentés par lui-même (printed in 1931 but not put on sale until
1933), they were accompanied by marginal notes, written in
1929–1930, and giving Valéry's later attitude toward his earlier
writings on the subject.[11] Valéry also wrote two shorter essays
on Leonardo, "L'Œuvre écrite de Léonard de Vinci" (published
in the Figaro, May 13, 1939) and a preface to a publication of
the Carnets de Léonard de Vinci (1942).[12]

How and when did Paul Valéry become fascinated by the
figure of Leonardo da Vinci? It must have been at a relatively
early age, at least while he still lived in Montpellier, since in a
curious passage of a letter to André Gide, dated January 3, 1895,
he says that he had "seen" Vinci's Flying Man in or near Montpellier. After touching on the difficulties he was encountering in
writing his article on Leonardo for the Nouvelle Revue (his
ironic and disillusioned tone is characteristic of the always over-
modest way in which he referred to his own writings—not only
then but later), he continued thus:

What an error! To have to shape to this format the great Flying Man. How many times, from the Peyrou,[13] I have seen him crossing from the sea to the west, shattering the circles of the delicate sky. He was making his test flights—in the air, in his machine which had become inseparable from him—but in reality, it was as if it were *myself*. Was it to teach me to read? What an alphabet! Something that even if it becomes emmired is still at the tops of the trees. (*Corresp. Gide-Valéry*, p. 229.)

In the article of 1939, referred to above, Valéry told of his discovery of the notebooks of Leonardo:

I was about twenty when in a Library where I went occasionally to kill time, chance made me open and leaf through one of the volumes of the photographic reproduction of the manuscripts of Leonardo, one of those published by Ravaisson-Mollien from the originals which belong to the Institute. I hadn't imagined up to then that there existed in the world such an extraordinary document on the mental life of a mind of the first rank, and on its intimacy with power. . . . These notebooks of Leonardo's were absolutely for himself alone, his laboratory of secret investigations. He wrote down in them only what could be useful to him in the development of his own resources.[14]

Is it necessary to point out the analogy between Valéry's interpretation of the basic function of Leonardo's notebooks and the basic function of his own *cahiers*?

I think it possible (though I have no proof) that Paul Valéry's early interest in Leonardo may well have been confirmed by a reading of Gabriel Séailles' *Léonard de Vinci*, which appeared in 1892.[15] It includes a biography, studies of Leonardo as scientist and as artist, and (as I shall point out below), in the conclusion there is a sentence which sums up very well what was Valéry's own conception of the significance of this man of genius. It also furnished detailed bibliographical information on the manuscripts of Leonardo.

If, as I assume, Valéry read Séailles' book, he must surely have been struck by a sentence such as this: "The life of Leonardo de Vinci shows that reflexion and imagination are not mutually exclusive, that a great artist can also be a great *savant*, and that these opposed qualities, by their coexistence, can raise the *savant*

and artist to an extraordinary height." [16] Monsieur Teste, who
at least in the preliminary form of Auguste Dupin was conceived
before Valéry wrote his first study of Leonardo, represented the
powers of reflexion pushed to an extreme, but without the
creative imagination of the artist. Leonardo represented both,
and was thus close to the young Valéry's ideal. In 1919 he re-
called his attitude of 1894 toward Léonardo: "I felt that this
master of his own resources, this possessor of draftsmanship, of
images, of mathematics, had discovered the central attitude based
upon which the enterprises of the understanding and the operations of art are equally possible . . ." ("Note et digression"—
Œuvres, I, p. 1201.) And, twenty-three years later, in his preface
to the Carnets of Leonardo, he expressed even more explicitly
his conception of the unique greatness of the Italian master:
"There was once someone who was able to look at the same spectacle or the same object, first as a painter would have looked at
it, then as a naturalist, then as a physicist, and on other occasions
as a poet; and none of these glances was superficial." [17]

Among the various writings of Valéry on Leonardo da Vinci,
I would single out "Léonard et les philosophes" (1928—Œuvres,
I, pp. 1234–1269) as recommended, if not required, reading for
all professors of philosophy who teach esthetics. It is an effective
demolition of earlier philosophical concepts concerning the
"good," the "true" and the "beautiful."

None of these writings on Leonardo is in any way a biography.
In fact, as Valéry pointed out in a letter to André Gide, a letter
written while his first article on Leonardo was still in the stage
of gestation, when he showed what he had written to Marcel
Drouin (Gide's brother-in-law), the latter observed: "'that I was
not talking about Vinci.' I knew that only too well." (Letter of
February 4, 1895—Corresp. Gide-Valéry, p. 232.) In analyzing,
in a decidedly abstract way, the activity, the mental processes,
the mental and artistic stature of Leonardo da Vinci, Valéry was
really defining his own ideal—the Paul Valéry he would like to
be—and which his admirers now think he approached rather
closely.

III   The Socratic Dialogues and the Drama

The two preceding sections of this chapter were devoted to
the bases of the thought of Paul Valéry and to their expression:

in his notebooks and in the conception of the two figures who were the embodiments of the bases of his thought. In this section, I will be concerned with what were the byproducts of his meditation, the application of his meditations to various activities of man: I mean his "Socratic" dialogues and his dramatic dialogues entitled *Mon Faust*.

The first two of them, *Eupalinos ou l'architecte* and *L'Ame et la danse*, were written in the same year, 1921. In fact we know the exact date on which Valéry finished the second of these. In the *cahiers*, a note dated November 13, 1921, states "at 5:20 finished L'A. et la danse. Informed Gallimard." (*Cahiers*, vol. 8, p. 365.) He had probably begun this dialogue in July; at least a *cahier* written during that month contains, under the heading "Article: L'âme et la danse," some not very legible notes on the subject. (*Cahiers*, vol. 8, p. 198.) Both of these dialogues were commissioned works, and the very specific nature of the order for the first was (as we have seen) what determined the use of this form which Valéry was trying for the first time. In Chapter III, I discussed *Eupalinos* in some detail. *L'Ame et la danse* is a dialogue in which Socrates and Phædrus appear again, with a third character, Eryximachus, a doctor. These three figures (with several others) had appeared in one of Plato's finest dialogues, *The Symposium*. At the end of a banquet (in Valéry's dialogue) dancing girls come on the scene, and the three men comment enthusiastically. They are especially impressed by the leading ballerina, Athikté. In the course of the conversation, Socrates attempts to define the essential quality of the dance as an art form: "it is a flame, and as a flame it is analogous to the soul; whose 'business' is what has been, what will be, but never what *is*." (*Œuvres*, II, p. 171.) Valéry's own analysis of this dialogue (in a letter to Louis Séchan, who devoted a chapter of his book, *La Danse grecque antique*—Paris, 1930—to Valéry's work) is worth quoting:

The constant thought of the *dialogue* is physiological—from the digestive difficulties of the beginning to the final fainting-spell. . . . As for the form of the whole, I tried to make of the dialogue itself a kind of ballet of which the Image and the Idea are in turn the ballerinas. The abstract and the concrete lead by turns and are united in the final vertigo.

In a word, I didn't in any way observe historical or technical exacti-
tude (and for a good reason). I freely introduced what I needed to
keep my Ballet going and to vary the figures. This was applied to the
ideas themselves. Here they are *means*. It is true that this notion (that
ideas are *means*) is familiar to me and perhaps part of my *substance*.
It leads moreover to nasty thoughts with regard to philosophy (cf.
Léonard et les philosophes, which I published last year).[18]

Valéry continued by stating that he felt that Mallarmé's essay
on the dance was the last word on the subject, and for that reason
he had at first refused to write this dialogue ordered by the
Revue musicale. When he finally accepted the commission, he
included among the interpretations of the dance the one found
in Mallarmé's essay, which Valéry characterized as "prodigiously
written."

Mallarmé's *Divagations* (1897) include two essays on the dance,
of which that entitled "Ballets" (which appeared in the *Revue
indépendante* of December, 1886) is probably the one to which
Valéry was referring.[19] I must say that Mallarmé's article does
not seem to me "prodigiously written," and I do not find any
specific influence of it in Valéry's dialogue. Séchan, in his chapter
on *L'Ame et la danse*, in the book mentioned above, points out
that this dialogue is in no way an imitation of Plato's *Symposium*,
neither in the theory of the dance nor in the character of Socrates.
Valéry's Socrates is closer to Nietzsche—or to Monsieur Teste.

Although I used the title "The Socratic dialogues" for this
section, *L'Idée fixe*, the third of Valéry's dialogues, makes no
pretense at Greek coloration. Two men, "Edmond T . . ." (our
old friend, Monsieur Teste, somewhat humanized) and a doctor
of his acquaintance, both spending their vacation at the seashore,
meet by chance on the rocky coast and chat for an hour or so.
As I said above, Valéry's Socrates is not very close to Plato, and
we might even say that Edmond T. . . . and the doctor, of
L'Idée fixe are Socrates and Eryximachus in modern dress. The
style of this dialogue is of course different; I feel that in the
first two dialogues, Valéry, though avoiding exaggeration, used
a certain simplicity of language that seems "Greek" to us, whereas
the language of *L'Idée fixe* is definitely modern, though it avoids
triviality or slang. In the winter and spring of 1966, a considerable
number of Parisians were able to take note of the fact that, presented by two distinguished actors (Pierre Fresnay and Julien

Bertheau), a dialogue such as *L'Idée fixe* can be fascinating. (In fact the influential, if often bad-tempered, dramatic critic of the *Figaro*, Jean-Jacques Gautier, called it the leading dramatic event of the season.) As I indicated in Chapter IV, I find it impossible to say what the *subject* of this dialogue is. I repeat that I find it the brilliant byproduct of Paul Valéry's daily meditations. It also gives us some impression of Valéry as a conversationalist. All who knew the poet have testified to his brilliance in this respect. We have only fragmentary information about the charming conversation of Stéphane Mallarmé, which, unfortunately, was never written down. *L'Idée fixe* preserves for posterity a somewhat stylized, but I believe faithful, example of the way Paul Valéry must have talked.

Mon Faust, Valéry's only extant play, is placed, in the *Œuvres*, at the end of the dialogues. Since this work, or these works—*Lust* and *Le Solitaire* have in common only the characters of Faust and Mephistopheles—represent the only nonmusical dramatic work of Paul Valéry that went farther than a project, it may be justifiable to class it with the dialogues. And it is certain that the principal interest in these last (or nearly last) writings of Paul Valéry is the interchange of ideas, rather than the dramatic action, which, as I indicated when I mentioned *Mon Faust* in Chapter IV, leaves something to be desired. And yet Paul Valéry here made an effort at something more than a mere dialogue: in *Le Solitaire* there are spectacular effects, and in the third act of *Lust* there are *jeux de scène* of a pictorial nature. Since in Chapter IV, I summarized briefly the intrigue (if one can call it that) of *Lust*, I shall not repeat that here, but I shall make a few remarks about the characters, the situation, and the ideas expressed.

The hero: is he Paul Valéry, or Doctor Faustus, or both? He is of course, for the requirements of the plot, in part the traditional Faust, now aged for a second time and illustrious, but also anachronistically aware of the reasons for his fame ("hero of several esteemed literary and musical works" he qualifies himself—*Œuvres*, II, p. 283), and when he says he is beginning to doubt whether he had ever done business with the devil, Lust, his secretary, questions: "After three thousand performances?" (*Op. cit.*, p. 288.) But the situation of the aged master, Faust, dictating to his attractive young secretary, Lust, "the young lady of crystal," makes one wonder whether this is not a portrayal of a real-life situation: the sixty-nine-year-old Valéry with a young secretary toward whom his feelings are somewhat mixed. But if Valéry is portraying himself in a real-life situation of 1940, he is doing it with an amusingly self-conscious irony. His Faust is not only in part the traditional character, in part Valéry himself, he contains also a satirical portrayal of the "great man"—genius, philosopher, writer—that Valéry felt he himself was not and had never wanted to be. Could he, in having Faust describe the sort of work he wanted to write, have been thinking of one or more of his distinguished contemporaries?

But I wish to give the strongest, the most poignant impression of sincerity any book has ever produced, and this powerful effect can be obtained only by loading oneself with all the horrors, intimate ignominies or execrable experiences—true or false—which a man can think of. There is nothing so vile or so stupid which doesn't give a color of truth to an autobiography. (*Œuvres*, II, p. 286.)

Was Valéry thinking of Gide's autobiographical writings? Years before (*Choses tues*, 1930) he had expressed skepticism as to the usefulness of sincerity: "Intentional sincerity leads to reflexion, which leads to doubt, which leads to nothing." (*Œuvres*, II, p. 494.)

The character of the Disciple, who comes to worship the Master, and hopes to obtain wisdom and inspiration from him, only to be rebuffed, may be based in part on similar young men who presumably pestered Valéry, but has points of resemblance with Valéry himself, as he was at the age of twenty. The Disciple, like Valéry—who at that age wished to destroy all the "idols" (*Propos me concernant*, 1943—*Œuvres*, II, p. 1510), is already disillusioned; Mephistopheles tries to tempt him, but does not succeed; the things he offers do not interest the young man.[20] And when the tempter offers him Faust's libary, a huge library containing all the scholarship in the world, the Disciple characterizes it as the "monumental edifice of the UNREADABLE." (*Œuvres*, II, p. 364.) Valéry himself said, in 1943: "I hardly like to read for the sake of reading. In the matter of literature, I pay attention to little but the forms and the composition; the rest never seems to me to be serious, that is, worth absorbing." (*Propos me concer-*

nant—Œuvres, II, p. 1511.) I hardly dare to suggest that the situation of Faust and the eager worshipping Disciple is a reflexion of Valéry's own relation to Stéphane Mallarmé. Valéry worshipped Mallarmé; he was certainly not rebuffed by the older master; they became friends, and Valéry was a frequent visitor, not only at the Tuesdays of the rue de Rome but also at Mallarmé's country home in Valvins. But maybe this relationship was too superficial to satisfy the author of the "Cimetière marin"; he later complained that Mallarmé's untimely death had prevented them from having the heart-to-heart talk about fundamental things that Valéry hoped to have.[21]

Humor, sometimes subtle, sometimes less so, is not lacking in *Lust.* The basic situation—an aged philosopher in love with, or at least having a feeling of tenderness for, his young secretary—is not without humorous or possibly ridiculous potentialities. Faust is somewhat aware of this himself; Mephistopheles and his subordinate demons even more so. Faust is fascinated by the term "Eros énergumène" (Eros possessed of a demon) which Lust reads to him from his notes and which he discovers had been slipped into them by the devil. The Master's only advice to the Disciple is "Prenez garde à l'amour" (watch out for love). When the play opens, Lust, the secretary, is in the midst of a spell of uncontrollable laughter, and we learn later that it was caused by the term "convulsion grossière" (crude convulsion), which Faust had applied to two functions of the body, laughter and vomiting, but for which a sexual implication is obvious. The term is taken up by Mephistopheles and his demons and is repeated, with sneers or mocking laughter, at intervals, becoming a sort of *leit-motif.* Mephistopheles' comment on the relation between Faust and Lust is brief and to the point: "The little chick is really caught. But the gallant is no longer very sharp." (*Œuvres,* II, p. 332.)

As early as "Ebauche d'un serpent" and "La Pythie," [22] Valéry had shown a tendency toward humorous parody of well-known quotations. This tendency recurs at intervals in the *cahiers,*[23] comes occasionally to the surface in the selections from them composing *Tel quel,* and is very effectively present in the *Lust* section of *Mon Faust.*

Pascal was Valéry's special *bête-noire;* in the *cahiers* his name or one or another of his *pensées* come up frequently to be ridiculed or refuted. The *pensée* to which Valéry devoted an article in the early twenties, "le silence éternel de ces espaces infinis m'effraie" (the eternal silence of these infinite spaces frightens me), is his particular butt, and he took special pleasure in composing parodic variations on it: see *Cahiers*, vol. 6, p. 671, vol. 10, p. 749, also *Autres Rhumbs—Œuvres*, II, p. 696. One of these is found in *Lust;* horrified by the spectacle of Faust's library, the Disciple exclaims: "The eternal silence of these innumerable volumes frightens me." (*Œuvres*, II, p. 365.) The other parody of Pascal is less obvious; the Disciple has just remarked: "I am saying absurdities." Mephistopheles replies sententiously: "The absurd has its reasons, Sir, which the reason suspects" (*Œuvres*, II, p. 355). (Cf. Pascal: "Le coeur a ses raisons que la raison ne connaît pas"—the heart has its reasons which the reason does not know.) The other allusion to Pascal is merely allusion (and implied criticism) and not parody. It is a reference to the *pensée:* "Tu ne me chercherais point si tu ne m'avais trouvé" (you would not be seeking me—God is addressing the Christian—if you hadn't found me). To Valéry this is for the conformist merely a reassurance of his own conformity; and that is how Mephistopheles alludes to it (speaking to the Disciple): "You brought here a mind which was disposed to hear only what it had promised itself it was going to hear. That's the disadvantage of seeking (as someone has said) only what one has already found." (*Œuvres*, II, p. 316.)

The other parodic allusions are not tendencious; Valéry was merely having fun. Shakespeare's "to be or not to be" appears in the form "to have duration or not to have duration that is nevertheless the question" (*Œuvres*, II, p. 365), and Buffon's famous and much-discussed definition "le style c'est l'homme même" (style is the man himself) is metamorphosed, in a brief discussion between Faust and Mephistopheles on the question of the style of the former's projected *magnum opus*, into "le style c'est le diable" (style is the devil) (*Œuvres*, II, p. 298).[24]

As I said in Chapter IV, the second part of *Mon Faust, Le Solitaire*, seems to me less interesting than *Lust*. For one thing, it is more fragmentary. It is true that only three acts out of four of *Lust* were completed, but these three acts contain enough dramatic action, interesting situations and witty dialogue to make a play, and a play that was given successfully for months in 1962.

The two existing acts of *Le Solitaire* leave us rather in the dark as to what is happening, though the final words seem to me typical of Valéry's essentially negative attitude toward the world:

FIRST FAY
But if we control all nature,
It is as slaves of words mysterious to us:
He who possesses them reigns and commands our actions.
The Word has power over the Metamorphosis,
You should know that who know all.

FAUST
Do I know one of these words?
SECOND FAY
You know only how to deny.
FIRST FAY
Your first word was NO. . . .
SECOND FAY
Which will be the last.
(*Œuvres*, II, pp.402–403.)

In the first act of this "dramatic fantasy," Faust and Mephistopheles have climbed far above the world to a region of glacial peaks. There Mephistopheles, who suffers from mountain sickness ("le mal des sommets"), leaves Faust and goes back down. The latter comes upon a creature entitled "Le Solitaire" (the Lonely One), a violent, cynical sort of superman, presented as superior to both Faust and Mephistopheles. Faust says: "He is rigorously mad. Fundamentally much worse than the devil. This madman is much further advanced." (*Œuvres*, II, p. 385.) He resents Faust's presence and bids him begone. Though Faust hides behind a rock, the Lonely One finds him and hurls him into the Abyss. Who or what is this Lonely One? Whereas Faust here represents the average intelligent man, endeavoring to know all by acquisition of learning, and Mephistopheles the conventional conception of "evil," *Le Solitaire* seems to be a sort of Super-Teste, a man or being led by his supreme intelligence to complete negation, to nihilism, and even dehumanization: "It is the hour, it is the time for me to change into a wolf!" says he. (*Œuvres*, II, p. 391.)

In the second part of this work (the first part was "Premier

Acte," the second is called "Intermède"—interlude), Faust has
fallen into some sort of grotto, where he is surrounded by fays,
who bring him back to life with a kiss. The dialogue, which contains some poetry demonstrating that the old poet had not lost
the control of his medium, is inconclusive—natural enough in the
case of an interlude. As I indicated (see the quotation given
above), what conclusion there is is negative. Is Faust fundamentally as much a nihilist as the Lonely One? Possibly, but he
is not as violent.

IV Paul Valéry, Critic of Criticism, of Critics, Writers and Literature

Paul Valéry wrote many literary articles; some of them were
prefaces for new editions of works of writers of different periods:
La Fontaine, Montesquieu, and Stendhal are examples. Others
were first given as lectures. Still others were commemorating
speeches. The wide variety of authors represented suggests no
pattern of personal choice, but rather the chance of commissions
given the poet. Can we call this literary criticism? Hardly, though
from the point of view of literary theory and literary history, most
of the material in these studies is of interest. Those to which I
am referring[25] are printed in the Œuvres, section "Variété," heading "Etudes littéraires," and they amount to more than 350 pages
(Œuvres, I, pp. 427–784, and notes, op. cit., pp. 1704–1755). It
is obviously impossible to discuss all of these here. For one thing
not all of the "prefaces" deal with literary criticism or literary
history. The preface to Montesquieu's Lettres persanes, for instance, is mainly sociology; it is an original and profound if somewhat abstract study of eighteenth-century French society. A
rather detailed analysis of Valéry's published literary articles is
to be found in Maurice Bémol's La Méthode critique de Paul
Valéry (Paris, 1950), to which I refer the reader. As a literary
critic (rather than an author of prefaces on literary figures)
Valéry can best be studied in the cahiers and in the extracts
from them published in Tel quel and elsewhere.

The paradox exists that, as we have seen, Valéry, considered
during his lifetime and still now as a great writer, was hostile
to the idea that he was himself a writer; he was equally hostile
to literature as a profession, as a mode of life. Was he—at that
time friendly with the writers who were to become the leaders

of the Surrealist movement—responsible for the fact that they entitled their review *Littérature,* which was of course meant in the same sense as the contemptuous final verse of Verlaine's "Art poétique": "Et tout le reste est littérature?" [26]

Whereas Valéry never made a statement to the effect that literature was worthless, he did consider it fundamentally *impure,* and he explained why:

There is always in literature something equivocal: the fact that a public must be kept in mind. Therefore there are always reserves in one's thoughts, a hidden intention in which is to be found a whole stock of charlatanism. Therefore every literary product is an *impure* product. (*Cahier B 1910—Œuvres,* II, p. 581.)

Poetry interested him more than other forms of literature, and he was particularly severe in his judgment of poetry in general. Silliness and stupidity (*niaiserie et sottise*) were its chief vices. In 1923 he wrote:

If poetry must accept silliness, if it must be measured on the basis of the capacity of inferior minds, if Musset is what satisfies you, if a poet is allowed to use crude means (*moyens*), if a mosaic of images is a poem, then to hell with poetry. (*Cahiers,* vol. 9, p. 591.)

And a little later he said:

The great stumbling block for poets is stupidity, silliness. Another stumbling block immodesty or impudicity—lay bare one's own vulgarity, cash in on the vulgarness of oneself. Musset, etc., "the most desperate. . . ."[27] (*Cahiers,* vol. 9, p. 687.)

Valéry was very severe in his judgment of his contemporaries, the poets whom he had known in his youth, as this statement (1897?) in the first volume of his *cahiers* shows:

I have known many poets. Only one[28] was what he was supposed to be or what I like. The rest were stupid or flat or of an unwavering cowardice of mind. Their impotence, their vanity, their childishness, and their grandiose, disgusting refusal to see clearly things as they are, their superstitions, their glory, their terrible resemblance to no matter whom, and, as soon as the task is done, their mental servility.

Finally, they bear all the chains of language, which makes them in the present-day world villagers, provincials. All that independent of literary talent, which can coexist perfectly with the most extreme stupidity. (*Cahiers*, vol. 1, p. 193.)

Nearly thirty years later (1924), he discussed in general terms what to do about stupidity and poetry:

Stupidity and poetry. Whether a man with an active mind can bear reading poetry? Isn't he obliged to fail to make use of his powers? To pretend? How can he digest the silliness, etc.? Occasionally a delightful detail, but at what a price! We poets are forced to be stupid, to say in verse what is unthinkable in the light of common sense. It was necessary then to change the whole system. Effort to make a non-stupid poetry. (*Cahiers*, vol. 10, p. 439.)

How this effort to make "nonstupid" poetry worked out will be seen below, where I reveal some of Valéry's opinions concerning individual poets and the evolution of French poetry.

A second facet of Valéry's literary theories was his hostility to literary critics. This stemmed partly from his conviction that individually they were incapable, but also from his general objection to the critical methods in use. He made the following severe general judgment in 1928:

Parasitism of critics. They are beings who cannot exist or subsist except by the negation of other beings. They would perish without those on whom they live by criticizing them. They are recognized by the nullity of their positive accomplishments. (*Cahiers*, vol. 12, p. 737.)

Two notes in the spring of 1921 attack not only Brunetière (now discredited, not only as a critic but also as a historian of literature, but then respected, at least in the United States) but also Taine and Sainte-Beuve. The first is the project of an article on critics (never to be written):

"The story of Brunetière, uninterested in poetry (according to his confession to Heredia, who related it to me) and judging poets. (And that continues)." (*Cahiers*, vol. 7, p. 861.) The second note is more sweeping:

"Whether it is a question of Taine or Brunetière or Sainte-

Beuve or others, these gentlemen are not useful; they have nothing to say. They are wordy mutes. They don't even suspect what their real subject is." (*Op. cit.*, p. 881.)

But Valéry's scorn for critics was best expressed in an aphorism of 1917 (inspired by some slighting remarks on *La Jeune Parque*?): "Critics. The dirtiest cur can inflict a mortal wound; all he needs is to be *mad*." (*Cahiers*, vol. 6, p. 652—reproduced in *Rhumbs—Œuvres*, II, p. 634.)

Though Paul Valéry and Marcel Proust were, as writers, as thinkers, as human beings, at opposite poles, they were in agreement on one point: their basic hostility to the biographical method in criticism. Proust's *Contre Sainte-Beuve* is more detailed, but Valéry is equally incisive:

"Criticism. Biography and even bibliography cause the real problems to disappear: as if one deduced from the dimensions of the ship the age of the captain—or rather it is just the opposite that they do." (*Cahiers*, vol. 12, p. 431—1927.) Ten years later, in a lecture on "Villon and Verlaine," he expressed the same opinion at greater length:

I feel—and that is one of my paradoxes—that the knowledge of the biography of poets is a useless bit of knowledge, if it is not harmful to the use which one should make of the poet's works, and which consists either of enjoyment or profiting from the information or the artistic problems which we derive from them. What do I care about Racine's love affairs? It is *Phèdre* that interests me. . . . And if I say that biographical curiosity can be harmful, it is because too often it furnishes the opportunity, the pretext, the means of avoiding the precise and organic study of a certain poetry.[29] (*Œuvres*, I, p. 428.)

On a few occasions the skeptical Valéry suggested that complete relativism in matters of literary judgment was a possibility. In one of his conversations with Frédéric Lefèvre (published in 1926), à propos of the stanza form used in his odes, he denied that it came from Jean-Baptiste Rousseau:

I don't know that poet as well, perhaps I know him less well than those who compare me to him and who surely never read him. But he *was* once a very great poet and it is not impossible that he become one again. (Quoted in *Œuvres*, I, p. 1646.)

In the same year in which the *Entretiens* with Lefèvre were published, Valéry devoted most of his little preface, "Oraison funèbre d'une fable" (preface to a new edition of La Fontaine's little-known fable, "Daphnis et Alcidamure") to a somewhat melancholy discussion of the decline and death of works of literature:

Between the fullness of life and the final death of works still in existence materially there passes a time which produces an imperceptible degradation, which alters them by degrees. . . . They witness the disappearance, one by one, of all their chances of pleasing. . . . And everything ends up in the Sorbonne. [That is, becomes merely of historical interest, and an object of erudite study.] (*Œuvres*, I, pp. 497–498.)

The preceding pages may have suggested that the skeptical Valéry was purely negative in these questions. That is not entirely the case: he had a positive conception of the function of criticism, and he made definite judgments regarding not only individual writers, but also regarding the evolution of French literature, and especially—as was natural—of French poetry.

A page of analysis of the function of the critic appeared in *Choses tues* (1930). The following is the essential paragraph:

Criticism to the extent to which it is not limited to giving opinions according to its own mood or taste—that is, talking about itself while imagining that it is talking about a literary work—criticism, to the extent that it *judges*, consists of a comparison between what the author intended to do and what he has done in reality. While the *value* of a work is a singular and not constant relation between the work and some reader, the exact and intrinsic *merit* of the author is a relation between himself and his plan: this merit is relative to the distance between these; it is measured by the difficulties that one found in carrying out one's enterprise. . . . A criticism which would be ideal would judge uniquely on the basis of this merit, since you can only require a person to accomplish what he proposed to accomplish. (*Œuvres*, II, pp. 479–480.)

The critic can properly ask the author the following questions:

You wanted to write a certain book? Did you do it? What was your plan? Did you have the intention of adhering to a noble thought or some perceptible advantage: a victory over opinions, a good financial success? . . . Whom did you wish to divert? Whom were you aiming to seduce, to equal, to make mad with envy? What head were you hoping to make pensive or to haunt for several nights? Tell us, Milord Author, is it Mammon or Demos, Cæsar or God whom you were serving? Venus perhaps or maybe all of them? (*ibid.*, p. 480.)

If these statements and questions do not seem to represent very new or different principles of criticism,[30] let us remember that, basically, Valéry's attitude was, as always, very rigorous. Let us also remember a statement that I quoted at the beginning of this chapter:

Poe was the first to think of giving a purely theoretical basis to literary works. Mallarmé and myself. I think I was the first to try to avoid having any recourse at all to former notions—but to place everything upon a purely analytical basis. (*Cahiers*, vol. 12, p. 703.)

Neither in the *cahiers*, nor in the published articles will we find a systematic study of the history of French literature, but we will find certain constants in Valéry's opinions on French writers. There is abundant evidence to show that he had a very high regard for the great poets of the late nineteenth century— Baudelaire and the later Hugo (with reservations for both), Mallarmé (as expected), Rimbaud—and also Verlaine (he calls the latter three: "those three Magi kings of modern poetics"— *Œuvres*, I, p. 1281). One statement, in a *cahier* of 1917, is particularly sweeping: "Three-quarters of what is finest in French poetry was written between 1845 and 1885." (*Cahiers*, vol. 6, p. 748.) Since Valéry's opinions of these poets are fairly well known, I shall merely sum them up here.

His lecture of 1924, "Situation de Baudelaire," resumes not only his judgment as to the importance of Baudelaire, but also that of the importance of Victor Hugo. He found defects in each: an interesting note of 1913 compares the "sterility" of Mallarmé with the fecundity of Hugo: "H. is fecund, M. is sterile. But if everything that H. wrote had come into M.'s mind, he would have rejected 85% . . . This sterility is not nonproduction, it is nonacceptance." (*Cahiers*, vol. 4, p. 904.) But on the positive side, we have this, concerning Hugo:

But again, in the last period of his life, what prodigious verses, verses to which, in extent, in internal organization, in resonance, in plentitude, no others can be compared! In *La Corde d'Airain,* in *Dieu,* in *La Fin de Satan,* in the poem on the death of Gautier, the septuagenarian artist, who had seen the death of all his rivals, who had been able to see a whole generation of poets born from him, and who was even able to profit from the exceptional lessons that the disciple can give the master if the master survives, the illustrious old man reached the highest point of poetic power and of the noble discipline of the versi-fier. ("Situation de Baudelaire"—*Œuvres,* I, p. 603.)

Valéry was at times severe in his judgment of Baudelaire's poetry—inasmuch as details were concerned: "In Baudelaire there are six verses out of ten which are of no value and which are verses only in the context of the conventions of Boileau and arbitrary rules." (*Cahiers,* vol. 7, p. 863—1921.) But here is his definitive, general judgment: "I can say that if there have been among our poets, poets who were greater and more powerfully endowed than Baudelaire, there have been none who were more *important.*" ("Situation de Baudelaire"—*Œuvres,* I, p. 598.) Valéry goes on to explain that, even leaving aside the great in-trinsic value of much of the poetry of Baudelaire, he is important from three points of view: 1. for causing French poetry to have an international diffusion and prestige (*rayonnement*—a difficult word to translate)—he refers to Swinburne, Gabriele D'Annun-zio and Stefan Georg; 2. for having discovered Poe and profited by his lessons; 3. for having engendered several very great poets.

Paul Valéry's permanent and unwavering admiration for the poetry of Stéphane Mallarmé, which equalled his permanent de-votion to the memory of the man himself, is so well known that I feel it is unnecessary to elaborate. The section of the *Œuvres* taken from the volumes of *Variété* contains some 100 pages of text and twenty pages of notes on various aspects of Mallarmé's life and works; and references, allusions, and critical notes con-cerning Mallarmé are frequent in the *cahiers.*

The case of Rimbaud is more complex. Valéry never devoted a lecture or an article to the author of the *Illuminations.* But in-stances of his high rating of Rimbaud are numerous. In 1925 he indicated that at about the age of nineteen the impact of Rim-baud upon him was considerable; so great that he disdained another important poet whose work appeared in the same year

(1891). In answer to an inquiry the results of which were published in the review *Le Disque vert*, under the title "Le Cas Lautréamont," he said:

Do I dare to confess to you that I scarcely know him [Lautréamont], if it is knowing him at all to have leafed through, ages ago, a copy of the *Chants de Maldoror?* It seems to me that I can explain why I didn't push my curiosity deeper into that work; I was nineteen,[31] and I had just received the little volume of the *Illuminations*.[32]

It is generally believed, on the basis of a letter from Valéry to Gide dated 1908, that the author of "Le Cimetière marin" recanted, at least inasmuch as the "Bateau ivre" was concerned. In a letter of August, 1891 (presumably preceding his discovery of the *Illuminations*, which did not appear in volume form until November of that year), he had characterized the "Bateau ivre" as "admirable," (*Corresp. Gide-Valéry*, p. 116), but in 1908, he said that, in reading the poem to the painter Degas, "as I recited my 'Bateau,' I found it sillier and sillier, that is, the boat. . . . The *Illuminations* remain, I think." (*Corresp. Gide-Valéry*, p. 417.) I shall point out that this reaction does not seem to have been lasting; four years later, in one of his *cahiers*, under the heading, "Rimbaud *prophet*," he noted down, with obvious admiration, images from three widely-separated verses of the "Bateau ivre." (*Cahiers*, vol. 4, p. 727.)

Two articles in *Variété*, "*Passage de Verlaine*" (1921) and "Villon and Verlaine" (1937), bear explicit testimony to Valéry's admiration for the poet Paul Verlaine, coupled with wonder that such a sordid individual could have been a great poet:

How can one imagine that this hobo, sometimes so brutish in appearance and in words, sordid, inspiring at the same time alarm and compassion, was nevertheless the author of the most delicate poetic music, of the newest and most touching verbal melodies that exist in our language? ("Villon et Verlaine"—*Œuvres*, I, p. 440.)

The judgment expressed by Paul Valéry with regard to the French seventeenth century in general and to some of its most admired writers in particular will be startling to many. The "baseness" (*bassesse*) of the seventeenth century, and the "ignoble" Molière, Pascal and La Fontaine: these judgments recur fairly frequently, especially in the twenties (see, for instance, *Cahiers,* vol. 12, p. 104—1927—and vol. 13, p. 103—1928). Valéry did not condemn all of seventeenth-century French literature. His admiration for Racine's poetry, and the influence of that poetry on *La Jeune Parque* are well known, as I pointed out earlier; his fine article on La Fontaine's *Adonis* revealed him as an admirer of at least one aspect of La Fontaine's work. But we saw earlier that Valéry, as he explained it himself, did not appreciate Racine until his late thirties.[33] And this appreciation must have been much more for the poet than for the dramatist. I discovered, with considerable surprise, a note in the *cahiers* dated "7.11.27" which reveals that when he saw and heard *Bajazet,* played by the "Petite Scène," it was the first time he had been present at the performance of a Racine tragedy. (*Cahiers,* vol. 12, p. 462.) He was then fifty-six. And the admiration that he felt for some of La Fontaine's work did not extend to all of it, for he said in 1918: "The verse of La Fontaine goes from the finest music to the most formless prose." (*Cahiers,* vol. 7, p. 66.)

Valéry's objection to the seventeenth century was not to classicism *per se,* which he discussed in some detail and not unfavorably in the selection of notes published in 1929 under the title *Littérature* (*Œuvres,* II, pp. 563–565), but the tendency of its typical representatives—Boileau, Molière, La Fontaine and Pascal—to be what he calls "ignoble." These notions of *bassesse,* of *ignoble,* are merely one more manifestation of Valéry's custom of thinking things through, of his refusal to accept conventional critical *clichés.* The ideal of the Golden Mean, and that "perfect reason avoids all extremes" (Molière, *Le Misanthrope*), these were not acceptable to Valéry. These ideals (or principles) seemed to him a demonstration of the servility imposed by Louis XIV; the campaign to reduce the power and the independence of the nobility implied crushing what was "noble" in man, and imposing a *bourgeois* ideal of mediocrity. His most general statement along these lines was made in 1927:

Seventeenth Century—Century of Baseness.
Louis XIV busied in reducing the most prominent people in the kingdom to the state of servants—putting them at an infinite distance from him. Twilight of the aristocracy whereby Colbert and Molière are elevated. Molière—origin of rationalizing janitors. He says "What-

ever is beyond my comprehension is the enemy of the human race."
All writers in servitude. Hypocrisy, forms. Nullity of thought from
1670 to 17. . . . The existence of Louis XIV during the time of
Spinoza hard to believe. (*Cahiers*, vol. 12, p. 104.) [34]

Valéry's curious use of the term "ignoble" applied to two pair-
ings: Molière and La Fontaine and Molière and Pascal, is illustrated by these two notes:

Molière and La Fontaine. Natural taste for the *ignoble*. One with men,
the other with animals. They were conspiring in their own ways
against the world of wigs, of enemas, of golden suns, of funeral ora-
tions and catafalques, in which they lived. (*Cahiers*, vol. 12, p. 575—
1927.)

Tableau of literature. I don't like Pascal or Molière. It's not a question here of their talents. I don't like the non-noble which is in them,
that is, the action on the lower faculties, which both of them wish to
torment; one by terror and disgust, the other by envy and depreciation
starting at the bottom. (*Cahiers*, vol. 13, p. 103—1928.)

V *Conclusion*

As we have seen, Paul Valéry abhorred literary critics and he
was really not one himself, but he was a *critic*, in the broadest
and most complete sense of the term. He had a critical mind,
which he applied to everything that came before him, disregard-
ing accepted principles or theories that did not stand up when
examined critically. This explains the unorthodox quality of
many of his judgments of writers, this explains his negative attitude toward history, this explains what seemed to be so original
and so profound in his view of contemporary events: he was not
afraid to face the facts, he then analyzed them, and formulated
simple, logical deductions from them in a way few other men of
his time dared to do or were capable of doing.

Valéry was one of the great thinkers of our times. And since
he expressed the results of his thinking in readable, clear and
forceful prose, he was one of the great prose writers of our time.

Notes and References

Chapter One

1. For most of the details of the biography I am indebted to the *Introduction biographique*, written by the poet's daughter, Agathe Rouart-Valéry, for the Pléiade edition of the *Œuvres* (*Œuvres de Paul Valéry, édition établie et annotée par Jean Hytier*, Paris, Gallimard, Bibliothèque de la Pléiade, 2 vols., 1957 and 1960), I, pp. 11–72. I shall henceforth refer to this edition as *Œuvres*.

2. Until 1928 the name was spelled "Cette."

3. And thus *French*, since Corsica had been French for over 100 years.

4. *Œuvres*, I, p. 47.

5. *Ibid.*, p. 13.

6. The notes to the *Introduction biographique* give as source of this merely "notes personnelles inédites" (unpublished personal notes)—see *Œuvres*, I, pp. 13–14, 1515.

7. This is reproduced in facsimile in Agathe Rouart-Valéry's *Paul Valéry*, Paris, 1966, p. 23. It is dated "mars 1884," when he was still going to school in Sète.

8. In *Précocité de Valéry*, Paris, 1957, pp. 47–48.

9. Quoted in *Œuvres*, I, p. 17.

10. Both were reprinted by Hytier in the Pléiade edition: "Le Jeune Prêtre," *Œuvres*, I, p. 1578; "Suave Agonie," *Œuvres*, I, pp. 1581–1582.

11. My quotations will be from this version, which is given in *Œuvres*, I, pp. 1551–1552. The version published in the *Album de vers anciens* of 1920 was not substantially changed. The earliest "Narcissus" of all written by Valéry was the irregular sonnet mentioned below (page 10) and dated September 28, 1890 (*Œuvres*, I, pp. 1555–1556). He retained very little of this sonnet in the *Conque* version (v. 1–4, 13), and made interesting revisions in those verses he did retain.

12. This is part of a talk given at Marseille in 1941—quoted in *Œuvres*, I, pp. 1557, 1558.

13. *Regards sur Paul Valéry*, Paris, 1951, p. 27.

14. Quoted in Œuvres, I, p. 1558.

15. J. Dubu, "Valéry et Courbet," *Revue d'Histoire littéraire de la France,* vol. 65, pp. 239–243, avril-juin 1965.

16. *Correspondance d'André Gide et de Paul Valéry,* Paris, 1955, p. 94.

17. Reprinted in Œuvres, I, pp. 1536–1537.

18. This verse was revised, as early as 1900, to read, "Innocente, et tu crois languir. Tu es éteinte." This produced a dying away effect, which was heightened in 1920 by the insertion of / . . . / after "languir."

19. On the date of this momentous event, see Œuvres, II, pp. 1433–1434.

20. I have not found the date or the place of publication of this letter (if it is published); a quotation from it is found in Octave Nadal's *A Mesure haute,* Paris, 1964, p. 152.

21. The same comments apply to this as to the preceding letter: see Nadal, *op. cit.,* pp. 152–153.

22. This event is alluded to rather mysteriously in two letters of December 1892 from Valéry to Gustave Fourment. See *Correspondance de Paul Valéry et de Gustave Fourment,* Paris, 1957, pp. 130–132 and also the explanations given by Octave Nadal in his notes (p. 236) and in his introduction (pp. 25–28).

23. On the other hand, Valéry's constant scorn for literature as a profession makes this interpretation doubtful. For a more *nuanced* explanation of this point, see my later discussion of *Eupalinos.*

24. "My last verses (*before the crisis*—my interpolation) very inferior to Mallarmé" he said in a letter of 1912 (or 1913) to Albert Thibaudet. (Quoted in Œuvres, I, p. 1731).

25. Two letters to Thibaudet, written in connection with the latter's book on Mallarmé, have been published a number of times: I quote from the Œuvres, I, p. 1730.

26. Though these *cahiers* have been reproduced *photographically* in volumes, they are really still *unpublished.*

27. "I am in the midst of *Eureka*" he wrote to Gide on March 3, 1892. (*Corresp. Gide-Valéry,* p. 150.)

28. *The French Face of Edgar Poe,* Carbondale, Ill., 1957, p. 269.

29. Some indication as to the real nature of the mind that decided this will be found in the last chapter of this book.

Chapter Two

1. For a further treatment of the *cahiers* and of what they represented for Valéry, see Chapter 7, part 1.

2. These letters are reprinted in Œuvres, II, pp. 1460–1464.

3. See "L'Œuvre écrite de Léonard de Vinci," in *Vues*, Paris, 1948, p. 227.

4. See my article "The Date of composition of Valéry's *La Soirée avec Monsieur Teste*, *Modern Language Notes* LXXV, pp. 585–589, 1960.

5. *Ibid.*

6. See his letters to Gide of May-September, 1896 (*Corresp. Gide-Valéry*, pp. 264–281).

7. Quoted by André Breton in the 1924 *Manifeste du surréalisme*. See Breton, *Manifestes du surréalisme*, Paris, 1963, p. 15.

8. See the *Corresp. Gide-Valéry*, especially the letter to Gide of October 5, 1896 (p. 281).

9. *Commerce* was a deluxe literary review of which the three editors were Paul Valéry, Valery Larbaud and Léon-Paul Fargue. It was subsidized by Marguerite Caetani, Princess Bassiano and appeared between 1924 and 1932.

10. The dialogue "L'Idée fixe, ou deux hommes à la mer" (1932) contains what is, in my opinion, the most interesting reincarnation of M. Teste. See Chapter 4.

11. See the letter of August 30, 1906, to André Lebey—*Lettres à quelques-uns*, Paris, 1952, pp. 76–78.

12. A minor humoristic journalist of the period.

13. "Anne" was dated by Valéry "1893" (See *Œuvres*, I, p. 1568).

14. The first verse, instead of "Un feu distinct m'habite . . ." is "Le feu amour m'habite . . ."

15. On May 24, 1897, he wrote to Gide, from the Ministry: "Here we work all day long for seven mortal hours." (*Corresp. Gide-Valéry*, p. 297.) And when he had—temporarily, he believed, with a six months leave from the Ministry—taken up his duties as private secretary to Edouard Lebey, he feared being obliged eventually to return to the Ministry: "I feel that I will be prodigiously annoyed in having to return to that jail." (August 29, 1900, *op. cit.*, p. 370.)

16. *Valéry-Fourment Correspondance*, Paris, 1957, p. 156.

17. *Journal littéraire de Léautaud*, vol. I, Paris, 1951, p. 75.

18. *Corresp. Gide-Valéry*: "You know that the opinions of our excellent revolutionary comrades and friends have the gift of annoying and exasperating me." (Jan. 15, 1898, p. 308.)

19. See my article "Paul Valéry and the Emperor Tiberius," in *French Studies*, XLV, pp. 224–231, July 1960.

20. Over forty years later, in a conversation with Henri Mondor, Valéry mentioned her: "Bathilde, equestrienne in a circus. Her admirable muscle system kept its promises!" (Mondor, *Propos familiers de Valéry*, Paris, 1957, p. 258.)

21. *Corresp. Gide-Valéry,* p. 367.

22. Quoted in *Corresp. Gide-Valéry,* pp. 369–370.

Chapter Three

1. The publication of "Fée" was first revealed, I believe, by Jean Hytier, in *Œuvres,* I, pp. 1543–1544.

2. J. R. Lawler's article "The Technique of Valéry's 'Orphée'" in *Journal of the Australasian Universities Modern Language Association,* October, 1956, pp. 54–64, is excellent, but would have been even better if he had had access to the intermediate version of "Orphée" or to two intermediate manuscript versions which I have seen.

3. *Corresp. Gide-Valéry,* p. 423.

4. This must be the manuscript, entitled "P. A. Valéry, *Ses Vers,*" which Valéry presented to Gide in 1892, and which was published by Henri Mondor in *Les Premiers Temps d'une amitié,* Monaco, 1947.

5. In a *cahier* of June 1917 there is a note *"Comme j'ai fait la J. P.* Genèse—1912–1913–1914–1915–1916–1917" (*Cahiers,* vol. 6, p. 508.) This is a sure indication that *La Jeune Parque* was begun in 1912.

6. He wasn't.

7. There are some 800 pages of rough drafts, projects, etc., of *La Jeune Parque.*

8. In a brief essay entitled "Souvenir" (collected in *Mélange—Œuvres,* I, pp. 304–306) he discussed the question more philosophically: the writing of poetry (according to his own rigorous method) offered an escape from a disturbed world: "Dans certains états des choses de ma vie, il arriva que le travail de poésie me fut une manière de me séparer du 'monde.'" (*Loc. cit.,* p. 304.)

9. From Frédéric Lefèvre's *Entretiens avec Paul Valéry,* Paris 1926 —reprinted in *Œuvres,* I, p. 1612.

10. Charles Whiting's *Valéry jeune poète,* Paris, 1960, studies the early poems in their original form only.

11. *La Jeune Parque, manuscrit autographe, texte de l'édition de 1942, états successifs et brouillons inédits du poème, présentation et étude critique des documents par Octave Nadal,* Paris, Le Club de Meilleur Livre, 1957. (Now out of print, and impossible to find, except in libraries.)

12. There is some confusion over dates here. Valéry speaks of the *feuilleton* as if it had been written in the summer, but at the end of the essay he mentions that Pierre Louÿs had a personally annotated copy of the same thing, and December 1 is given as the date.

13. A curious case of how something completely unrelated could provide poetic stimulus for Valéry is this note in a *cahier* of 1914. "To-day March 17, 1914, I used profitably for a little verse job the excitement caused by a public scandal brought to my notice by the yells of

the newsboys. This cashing in of nervous credits is a general fact."
(*Cahiers*, vol. 5, p. 193.) The public scandal to which he referred was
surely the publication in the *Figaro* of Henriette Caillaux's letters. Two
days later Madame Caillaux shot Calmette, the editor of the *Figaro*.

14. But see note 33 to Chapter 7.

15. Jacques Duchesne-Guillemin, *Essai sur la Jeune Parque de Paul
Valéry*, Bruxelles, 1946, p. 55. This study and the even more useful
study of *Charmes* by the same author (Bruxelles, 1947) are both out of
print, but much of the material in them has been reprinted in the volume, *Etudes pour un Valéry*, Neuchâtel, 1964.

16. *Op. cit.*, pp. 66–76. In the more easily available *Etudes pour un
Valéry* (see preceding note) this "canevas chronologique" is given in
the appendices, pp. 225–237.

17. Elsewhere Valéry said (according to Gide's *Journal* for Jan. 2,
1923—Paris, 1939, p. 751) that the origin of "La Pythie" was the verse
(v. 5): "Pâle, profondement mordue" (pale, deeply bitten), which
came to him in his sleep. See also "Poésie et pensée abstraite" (*Œuvres*,
I, pp. 1338–1339.)

18. I shall discuss in (Chapter 6) the controversy over the "subject"
of *Charmes*.

19. This shows the versatility of Sorbonne professors. Gustave Cohen was primarily known as a medievalist.

20. I am referring to an interesting article entitled "An Interpretation
of Valéry's *Cimetière marin*," *Romanic Review*, April 1947, pp. 133–
158.

21. In 1914 he wrote to Gide (July 22), after passing through Sète,
"always beautiful and always more beautiful, the cemetery, with ole-
anders and cypresses." (*Corresp. Gide-Valéry*, p. 438.)

22. Valéry's letter to Doutenville, quoted above, contains the following details regarding the choice of the name *Eupalinos*: "The name
Eupalinos was found by me—I was hunting for an architect's name—
in the *Encyclopédie Berthelot*, in the article "Architecture." I learned
later, from the work of the learned Hellenist Bidez (of Ghent) that
Eupalinos was more an engineer than an architect, that he dug canals
rather then building temples; I gave him my ideas, as I did in the cases
of Socrates and Phædrus." (*Lettres à quelques-uns*, p. 215.)

23. Letter to M. Dupuy, quoted in *Œuvres*, II, p. 1401.

24. Letter to Doutenville—*Lettres à quelques-uns*, p. 215. In 1935
Valéry made the following revealing comment: "The little one knows is
sometimes more active and fertile than the much . . . The excessively
little that I knew of Plato, and which was limited to ten or fifteen *lines*,
produced *Eupalinos* for me." (*Cahiers*, vol. 18, p. 82.)

Chapter Four

1. Quoted, without reference, but probably from the *Cahiers*, in Agathe Rouart-Valéry's *Paul Valéry*, Paris, 1966, p. 167.

2. Those who cannot read these inscriptions in their place will find them reproduced in *Œuvres*, II, p. 1582.

3. It may have been the association, on the title page of *Commerce*, of the names Paul Valéry and Valery Larbaud that produced the amusing error that disfigured the generally accurate *Histoire illustrée de la littérature française*, edited by Bédier and Hazard. The chapter on the twentieth century was written by an obscure academician named André Chaumeix. He mentioned, among the distinguished writers of the century, Paul Valéry Larbaud!

4. The verses of the last section of the play, *Le Solitaire*, are more interesting. See Chapter 7, part III.

5. This title, a technical naval term, puzzled readers until Valéry explained it in an added preliminary note (*Œuvres*, II, p. 597.) The title might be paraphrased in English as "Tangential thoughts."

6. Agathe Rouart-Valéry, *Paul Valéry*, Paris, 1966, p. 115. For a reproduction of the sword, see p. 192.

7. See Henri Mondor, *Vie de Mallarmé*, édition en un volume, Paris, 1941, pp. 372–373.

8. See *Paul Valéry*, Bibliothèque Nationale, 1956, p. 3.

9. A note in *Autres Rhumbs*, taken from a *cahier* of 1922, mentions this (*Œuvres*, II, p. 686). See also my article, referred to above (Chapter 2, note 19).

10. *Mon Faust* (that is, *Lust, la demoiselle de cristal*) was played in 1962. *L'Idée fixe* was played (one hour and a half, without intermission) during the winter and spring of 1966. The presence, in both of these, of the great actor, Pierre Fresnay, was, at least, a partial explanation of their success. In two places it is stated that a performance of *Le Solitaire*, attended by Paul Valéry, was given in the spring of 1945 at the Comédie Française. According to the *Introduction biographique* it was April 17 (*Œuvres*, I, p. 72), whereas the notes in the Bollingen translation of Valéry's plays (Paul Valéry, *Plays*, New York, Pantheon Books, 1960—Bollingen Series XLV.3, p. 368) place the date as April 28. I looked through the file of *Carrefour* (a weekly to which Valéry had contributed) and the *Figaro*, but found no mention. The *Figaro* listed Comédie Française productions, and the only conceivable performance or reading of *Le Solitaire* might have been at a Saturday "matinée poétique." I found these announced for April 21 and May 12, but *not* April 17 or 28. It is true that paper was limited and the dailies and weeklies were miserably small at that moment.

11. It is surely not a mere coincidence that, after having presented

Le Neveu de Rameau in dramatic form in the season of 1963, Pierre Fresnay and Julien Bertheau decided to try the same thing with *L'Idée fixe*, in the 1966 season. They must have been aware of the analogy between the two works.

12. In October, 1926, Valéry gave a lecture in Vienna. See *Œuvres*, I, p. 50.

13. Jean Ballard published, in *Paul Valéry vivant, n. p.*, 1946, pp. 239–242, a few pages of *Faust*, which the poet wrote at Cassis (date not given) and which represent projects for completing the two plays. See *Œuvres*, II, pp. 1411–1414.

14. By Georges Le Breton, *Yggdrasill*, no. 9, December, 1937, to no. 35, February, 1939.

Chapter Five

1. Gide, *Journal*, Paris, 1939, p. 949. (Entry of October 28, 1929.)
2. Gide, *Journal*, Paris, 1939, p. 749. (Entry of December 30, 1922.)
3. *Situations II*, Paris, 1948, pp. 63–64.
4. *Op. cit.*, p. 87.
5. *Introduction à la poésie française*, Paris, 1939, p. 16.
6. This theory is of course similar to the "art for art's sake" principle expressed in Gautier's well-known poem, *L'Art*, though Valéry's formulation has more nuances. A page of the little preface entitled "De l'éminente Dignité des arts du feu" (*Œuvres*, II, p. 1241) contains a fine expression of this theory, but keyed to the plastic arts rather than to poetry.
7. Voltaire didn't put it in quite those words. He said, à propos of Corneille: "It is not *always* true that in our poetry there is *continually* one verse for the sense, another for the rime (italics mine)." (*Œuvres*, édition Moland, vol. XXXI, pp. 276–277.)
8. Taken from *Cahiers*, vol. 7, p. 406, 1919, but in the published form another sentence, the second, was added.
9. Valéry is referring to an untitled poem, which begins with the verse, "La servante au grand coeur dont vous étiez jalouse" (the greathearted servant of whom you were jealous) and continues with the verse "Et qui dort son sommeil sous l'humble pelouse" (And who sleeps her sleep under the humble lawn). These verses have been explained as alluding to Marie, the old maid-of-all-work to whom Baudelaire was devoted, which caused his mother to be jealous.
10. See my articles "La Nuit magique de Paul Valéry" in *Revue d'Histoire littéraire de la France*, vol. 60, pp. 199–212, avril-juin, 1960, and "New light on Valéry's *Féeries*" in *Modern Language Notes*, vol. LXXVI, pp. 755–756, December, 1961.
11. This long discussion of Valéry's poetic theory has been a bit abstract; a few concrete examples of how this poet labored over the con-

struction of a poem would have added more flesh. But I remember that this book is destined, among others, to many readers who are not bilingual. For them, detailed, concrete illustrations, often involving minor changes of meaning in French, would have been of little pertinence. To the bilingual reader, therefore, I recommend the following works, in which Valéry's processes of poetic composition have been well studied: Lloyd J. Austin, "Paul Valéry compose 'le Cimetière marin,'" *Mercure de France*, vol. 317, pp. 577–608, April 1953; vol. 318, pp. 49–72, May 1953. Octave Nadal, *La Jeune Parque de Paul Valéry*, édition critique, Paris, Club du Meilleur Livre, 1957.

Chapter Six

1. Valéry said this to Gide in December, 1922. (*Journal de Gide*, Paris, 1939, p. 749.)

2. In *Littérature*, the "Cantique des colonnes" appeared on the first page of the first number, March, 1919, and the "Ode secrète" was published in *Littérature* of February, 1920.

3. In March, 1921, *Littérature* published a curious poll in which eleven intellectuals of the dadaist group, most of whom became surrealists three or four years later, gave numbered plus or minus ratings to important figures of the period. Aragon, Breton, Soupault, and Drieu La Rochelle gave positive scores to Valéry; Eluard and Tzara were negative, the latter strongly so.

4. *Entretiens avec Frédéric Lefèvre*, 1926, quoted in *Œuvres*, I, p. 1646.

5. Fargue was never elected to the Académie française, nor was he, to my knowledge, ever a real candidate. For a number of years, as the first volume of Léautaud's *Journal* shows, he and Valéry saw each other very frequently. The passage I quoted is March 22, 1931—*Journal littéraire de Léautaud*, vol. 8, Paris, 1960, p. 342.

6. A symposium, "Valéry et nous," by four writers of this generation, Yves Bonnefoy, Jacques Charpier, Edouard Glissant and Jacques Howlett, appeared in *Lettres nouvelles* of September, 1958. Of the four only Bonnefoy seemed to have substantial reservations as to Valéry as a poet.

7. "Comment situer Valéry?" *Nouvelle Revue française*, February, 1960, pp. 311–312. Similar conclusions are to be found in Berne-Joffroy's *Valéry* (Paris, Gallimard, Bibliothèque idéale, 1960, pp. 134–137).

Chapter Seven

1. See, for instance, his letter to Jean de Latour, author of *Examen de Valéry* (Paris, 1935), quoted in *Œuvres*, II, p. 1499.

2. Vols. 1 and 2 in *Revue d'Histoire littéraire de la France* vol. 58

(1958), pp. 556–561 and vols. 3–10 in the same review vol. 60 (1960), pp. 245–259.

3. Analysis of vols. 22–29 of the *Cahiers* in *Revue d'Histoire littéraire de la France* vol. 63 (1963), pp. 62–89.

4. The notes on the first ten volumes have been reprinted (Paris, Editions Universitaires, 1964). Notes on vol. 11 and following have been appearing every five or six months in the *Revue de Paris*, from July 1964 on.

5. Judith Robinson, *L'Analyse de l'esprit dans les "Cahiers" de Valéry*, Paris, José Corti, 1963, p. 10.

6. *Lettres à quelques-uns*, pp. 244–245.

7. See the end of his "Fragment d'un Descartes" (*Œuvres*, I, p. 792.

8. In volume 10 of the *Cahiers* 9, p. 67), in a note dated June 24, 1924, he relates a conversation he had with Bergson.

9. Lettre au R. P. Gillet, January 30, 1927, in *Lettres à quelques-uns*, p. 163.

10. *Op. cit.*, pp. 13–22.

11. All of these writings are reprinted in *Œuvres* (I, pp. 1153–1269).

12. These two were reprinted in *Vues* (Paris, 1948), now out of print—and they were not included in the *Œuvres*.

13. The Peyrou is a park and waterworks, one of the showplaces of Montpellier, built in the late seventeenth century. André Gide and Paul Valéry both knew it well.

14. "L'Œuvre écrite de Léonard de Vinci" was reprinted in *Vues*. My quotation is page 227.

15. He himself says that some years after this early experience, he came upon *The Literary Works of Leonardo da Vinci*, edited and translated by Jean Paul Richter (an English art historian, not the German romantic), London, 1883, and was much impressed. See *Vues*, p. 229. This does not preclude his having read Séailles' work.

16. Gabriel Séailles, *Léonard de Vinci*, Paris, 1892, p. 509.

17. "Léonard de Vinci" in *Vues*, p. 217.

18. *Lettres à quelques-uns*, p. 190.

19. See *Œuvres de Mallarmé*, édition de la Pléiade, Paris, 1945, pp. 303–307.

20. Cf. the ironic version of the temptation of Adam, in *Mauvaises pensées et autres* (1941). Adam is not in the least interested in being like a god, and when he is offered the knowledge of good and evil, he says he would prefer to know something else. (*Œuvres*, II, p. 798).

21. See, for instance, this statement in a letter of 1942 to Henri Mondor: "Until the fatal summer of 1898, I continued to hope that

our increasing intimacy would allow me one day to speak to him in
person as I spoke to him in imaginary conversations. Note that, in
my mood of that period, a conversation of the type that I imagined
would have had for me a very great importance." (*Lettres à quelques-
uns,* p. 235.)

22. "Moi de qui relèvent les vampires" (I upon whom vampires
depend) in "Ebauche d'un serpent" is an ironic parody of Bossuet's
"de qui relèvent les empires," (upon whom empires depend) while
"Génie, cette longue impatience" in "La Pythie" is the parody of a
well-known definition of genius.

23. See his series of variations on "Je pense donc je suis" in *Cahiers,*
vol. 9, p. 783 (February, 1924), also same volume, p. 433 (1923).

24. I assume that the "Songe, songe, Satan" of Faust (think, think,
Satan) (*Œuvres,* II, p. 301) is a reminiscence of Andromaque's
pathetic cry to her *confidante:* "Songe, songe, Céphise . . ."

25. In addition to these, Hytier lists some twenty-six other prefaces,
most of which adorn the works of very obscure young poets.

26. Paul Valéry's "Cantique des colonnes" was the first work published in the first number of *Littérature.*

27. An allusion to Musset's well-known verses in *La Nuit de mai,*
"Les plus désespérés sont les chants les plus beaux, / Et j'en sais
d'immortels qui sont de purs sanglots." (The most desperate are the
most beautiful songs, / And I know some immortal ones which are
pure sobs.)

28. Obviously he means Mallarmé.

29. An example of this is a work by Emile Faguet in several
volumes entitled *Histoire de la poésie française,* but which would have
been better characterized by the title *Biographies des poètes français.*

30. J. E. Spingarn, in his *Creative Criticism* (1917) put it this way:
"What has the poet tried to do, and how has he fulfilled his intention?
What is he striving to express and how has he expressed it? What
impression does his work make on me, and how can I best express this
impression?" But Spingarn was just rewording what Carlyle had said
in characterizing Goethe's critical theory: "The critic's first and fore-
most duty is to make plain to himself 'what the poet's aim really and
truly was, how the task he had to do stood before his eye, and how
far, with such materials as were afforded him, he has fulfilled it.'"
(Quoted from *A Modern Book of Criticism,* edited by Ludwig
Lewisohn, New York, Modern Library, 1919, pp. 158–159.)

31. The volume to which he was referring was published late in
1891, so he was in reality twenty.

32. "Le Cas Lautréamont," *Le Disque vert,* 1925, pp. 93–94.

33. There is some conflict of evidence here. Pierre Féline, recalling,
a year after Valéry's death, his association with the poet in Montpellier

in the early 90's, says: "I tried to tease him about *his dear Racine*" [my italics] (*Paul Valéry vivant*, n. p., Cahiers du Sud, 1946, p. 45 n.) Had Valéry concealed from his friend his unorthodox lack of appreciation of Racine at that time, or is Féline's memory playing him tricks?

34. The only place in the *published* works where I noted a similar opinion is in the "Preface" to the *Lettres persanes* of Montesquieu. The time of Montesquieu was, according to Valéry, a good time to live because, among other things, "the Tartuffes, the stupid Orgons, the sinister officials, the absurd Alcestes were fortunately buried." (*Œuvres*, I, p. 513.)

Selected Bibliography

A complete bibliography of Paul Valéry (translations, books about Valéry, books to be consulted—for chapters or pages on Valéry—, articles) up to and including 1960, will be found at the end of the second volume of the Pléiade edition of Valéry's works (see below). Complete bibliographical information on individual works and on collected and selected works is to be found in the *notes* of the same edition. For the bibliography of Valéry *after* 1960, I recommend the *Year's Work in Modern Language Studies* (published annually by the Modern Humanities Research Association, Cambridge, England). This does not list all items, but it does indicate the importance of all items listed.

PRIMARY SOURCES

I. Collected and selected works, important editions, correspondence

Œuvres de Paul Valéry, edited by Jean Hytier. Paris: Bibliothèque de la Pléiade, Gallimard, vol. I, 1957, vol. II, 1960. Contains all of Valéry's important works (except the correspondence), barring the essays included in the volume *Vues* (Paris: La Table ronde, 1948). The justification for not including these essays—that they were easily available—if valid then, is no longer so; the book is out of print. The notes of the Pléiade edition are especially valuable; they contain not only variants and complete bibliographical information, but also many poems and essays not included in other editions, abundant quotations from the correspondence bearing on Valéry's opinions and theories, and, finally, listings of minor writings of various sorts not included in this edition.

Œuvres de Paul Valéry. Paris, 12 vols.: Le Sagittaire (vols. A and B), Gallimard (remaining volumes), 1931–1950. These handsomely printed quarto volumes, instead of being numbered, were identified by letters, as follows: A: *L'Ame et la danse, Eupalinos* (1931); B: *Monsieur Teste* (1931); C: *Album de vers anciens, La Jeune Parque, Charmes* (1933); D: *Variété I* (1934); E: *Discours* (1935); F: *L'Idée fixe* (1936); G: *Variété II* (1937);

H: *Pièces sur l'art* (1938); I: *Léonard de Vinci* (1938); J: *Regards sur le monde actuel* (1938); K: *Conférences* (1939); L: *Ecrits sur Mallarmé* (1950).

Poésies. Paris: Gallimard, 1942. This edition, often reprinted and still available, contains the *Album de vers anciens, La Jeune Parque, Charmes, Pièces diverses, Cantate du Narcisse, Amphion* and *Sémiramis.*

Poésies. Paris: Gallimard, 1966 (Collection: "Poésie"). Paperback format; omits *La Jeune Parque.*

Vues. Paris: La Table ronde, 1948. Essays not collected in Pléiade edition. Out of print.

La Jeune Parque. Edition critique, edited by Octave Nadal. Paris: Club du Meilleur Livre, 1957. Contains an extensive study of the work and its genesis, reproduction of original manuscript; pages and pages of manuscript variants. Out of print.

Cahiers. Paris: Centre national de la recherche scientifique, 29 vols., 1957–1961. A photographic reproduction, completed in 29 volumes, though 32 had originally been announced.

Lettres à quelques-uns. Paris: Gallimard, 1952. Does not contain any of the letters included in the two following items.

Correspondance d'André Gide et de Paul Valéry, préface et notes par Robert Mallet. Paris: Gallimard, 1955. Indispensable for students of Gide as well as Valéry.

Correspondance de Paul Valéry et Gustave Fourment, introduction et notes par Octave Nadal. Paris: Gallimard, 1957. Contains many hitherto unkown early poems of Valéry.

Charmes, précédés d'extraits en prose relatifs à la poétique de Valéry, edited by Robert Monestier. Paris, Larousse, 1958 (Classiques Larousse). Excellent introduction, good choice of extracts giving poetic theory; notes on the poems are clear and useful.

II. Translations of works into English

The Collected Works of Paul Valéry, ed. JACKSON MATHEWS. New York: Pantheon Books (The Bollingen Series XLV), 15 volumes, 1956—. Six volumes have appeared to date. Here is the list of projected volumes, with dates given after those that have already appeared: 1. *Poems;* 2. *Prose Poems;* 3. *Plays* (1960); 4. *Dialogues* (1956); 5. *L'Idée fixe* (1965); 6. *Monsieur Teste;* 7. *The Art of Poetry* (1957); 8. *Leonardo, Poe, Mallarmé;* 9. *Descartes, Goethe and others;* 10. *History and politics* (1962); 11. *Various occasions;* 12. *Degas, Manet, Morisot* (1960); 13. *Aesthetic Theory* (1964); 14. *Analects;* 15. *Moi and Bibliography.*

The Selected Writings of Paul Valéry, ed. ANTHONY BOWER and J. LAUGHLIN. New York: New Directions, 1950.

A list of translations of individual poems, through 1960, will be found in the Bibliography of the Pléiade edition of the *Œuvres,* II, p. 1638.)

SELECTIVE SECONDARY SOURCES

I. Books on Paul Valéry

ALAIN. *Charmes, poèmes de Paul Valéry commentés par Alain.* Paris: Gallimard, 1928. It was in reference to this, one of the first exegeses of Valéry, that the poet said "My verses have the meaning that one attaches to them."

BÉMOL, MAURICE. *Paul Valéry.* Clermond-Ferrand: G. de Bussac, 1949. This sizeable thesis (454 pp.), is the first important one to be devoted to the poet. It is a mine of information on Valéry's thought (minus, of course, the *Cahiers,* not then available). Less useful as a study of the poetry.

BENOIST, PIERRE-FRANÇOIS. *Les Essais de Paul Valéry, vers et prose.* Paris: Editions de la Pensée moderne, 1964. As the subtitle suggests, this is a general study (revival of the Mellottée series, "Les Chefs-d'Œuvres de la Littérature expliqués"). A few factual errors in the biography; explications of selected poems; selections from *Eupalinos* and *Mon Faust.*

BERNE-JOFFROY, ANDRÉ. *Présence de Valéry.* Paris: Plon, 1944. Contains Valéry's last autobiographical notes, "Propos me concernant" (reprinted in *Œuvres,* II, pp. 1505–1536).

————. *Valéry.* Paris: Gallimard (Bibliothèque Idéale), 1960. Probably the best general introduction to Valéry. Contains biography, brief study of works, selections from poetry and prose, an anthology of the poet's thoughts and opinions (brief statements) arranged in alphabetical order by subjects, an excellent bibliography, followed by "iconography," "musicography" and discography."

CAIN, LUCIENNE JULIEN. *Trois essais sur Paul Valéry.* Paris: Gallimard, 1958. Somewhat chaotic presentation of interesting analyses of Valéry's works and his thought.

COHEN, GUSTAVE. *Essai d'explication du "Cimetière marin."* Paris: Gallimard, 1933. The course given at the Sorbonne in 1928. Over-elaborate but generally sound interpretation. The preface is Valéry's important essay, "Au sujet du 'Cimetière marin.'"

DUCHESNE-GUILLEMIN, JACQUES. *Essai sur la Jeune Parque de Paul Valéry.* Bruxelles: L'Ecran du monde, 1946.

————. *Étude de Charmes de Paul Valéry.* Bruxelles: L'Ecran du monde, 1947. This and the preceding contain excellent analyses of these poems. Long out of print.

————. *Etudes pour un Paul Valéry*. Neuchâtel: A la Baconnière, 1964. This reproduces most of the first of the two preceding books and half of the other, with more recent essays added. Useful book.

GAÈDE, E. *Nietzsche et Valéry*. Paris: Gallimard, 1962.

HENRY, ALBERT. *Langage et poésie chez Paul Valéry*. Paris: Mercure de France, 1952. After a general study of the subject, there is a lexicon of the characteristic vocabulary used by Valéry in his poetry, with an indication for each word of its various shades of meaning in the poems in which it appears.

HYTIER, JEAN. *La Poétique de Valéry*. Paris: Armand Colin, 1953. Useful study, possibly over-systematic. Hurt by lack of mass of material in the *cahiers*, not then available.

INCE, W. N. *The Poetic Theory of Valéry*. Leicester: University Press, 1961. This book, written like the preceding, before the *cahiers* were published, was revised later and made some use of them, but not enough.

LA ROCHEFOUCAULD, EDMÉE DE. *En lisant les Cahiers de Paul Valéry*. Paris: Editions universitaires, 1964. Useful and readable guide to a work difficult of approach. Analyzes vols. 1–10. Others presumably will follow.

LAWLER, JAMES R. *Lecture de Valéry, une étude de "Charmes."* Paris: Presses universitaires, 1963. Contains first a brief, then an extensive discussion of each of the poems in *Charmes*. Mr. Lawler had access to much manuscript material not previously available, and made good use of it. Not everyone will accept all of his interpretations, but this is an essential book for the study of Valéry's poetry.

LECUYER, MAURICE A. *Etude de la prose de Paul Valéry dans "La Soirée avec Monsieur Teste."* Paris: Archives des Lettres modernes (no. 55), 1964. Detailed stylistic analysis (according to principles of Bally) of several short passages. Much of interest, but may seem inconclusive.

MACKAY, AGNES E. *The Universal Self, a study of Paul Valéry*. Toronto: University of Toronto Press, 1961. Contains not very relevant literary-historical material, a few factual errors. Reasonably readable and informative.

MONDOR, HENRI. *Précocité de Valéry*. Paris: Gallimard, 1957. Wordy (442 pp.) account of Valéry's childhood, youth, and early manhood. Contains unpublished very early poems (which Jean Hytier apparently did not consider worth reprinting in the *Œuvres*). Will be useful to Valéry specialists, who can discern the grain among the large amounts of chaff.

————. *Propos familiers de Paul Valéry*. Paris: Grasset, 1957. Often trivial, but sometimes very interesting conversations of Valéry, mostly at dinner parties. Also personal interviews with Mondor. Moving account of the latter's visits to Valéry in the weeks of the poet's last illness.

NADAL OCTAVE. *A Mesure haute.* Paris: Mercure de France, 1964. Six essays (out of twenty-two) in this book are devoted to Valéry. Enlightening.

Paul Valéry vivant. n. p. (Marseille?): Cahiers du Sud, 1946. A better than usual homage volume. Contains: a bibliographical introduction by Agathe Rouart-Valéry (now superseded by her biography in the *Œuvres*), tributes by friends (some very interesting), texts (now, I believe, all reprinted in the *Œuvres*), studies, and a bibliography of the "Cimetière marin."

Paul Valéry. Paris: Bibliothèque Nationale, 1956. This is the catalogue of the Valéry exposition of that year. It contains considerable information, not available elsewhere, about unpublished material.

PARISIER-PLOTTEL, JEANINE. *Les Dialogues de Paul Valéry.* Paris: Presses universitaires, 1960. Only general study of the dialogues.

ROBINSON, JUDITH. *L'Analyse de l'esprit dans les Cahiers de Valéry.* Paris: José Corti, 1963. Best discussion to date of what Valéry was trying to do in the notes he made on his daily meditations.

ROUART-VALÉRY, AGATHE. *Paul Valéry.* Paris: Gallimard, 1966. This is more than an iconographic documentation of Paul Valéry, his life, his work, his family, his friends. This handsome book, compiled by the poet's daughter, contains not only some 200 pages of portraits, reproductions of manuscripts and other documents, but also each reproduction is accompanied by pertinent texts of Valéry himself. (Only shortcoming: the source of these texts, not always obvious, is not indicated.)

SCARFE, FRANCIS. *The Art of Paul Valéry, a study in dramatic monologue.* London: Heinemann, 1954. This is not a general study, but a thesis, a very good one, both in the readable text and the discursive notes.

WALZER, PIERRE-OLIVIER. *La Poésie de Paul Valéry.* Geneva: Pierre Cailler, 1953. Still the best general study of Paul Valéry, the poet. Now out of print. With so much manuscript material having been since revealed, and the *cahiers* having been published, it is to be hoped that Walzer will do a revised edition.

WHITING, CHARLES F. *Valéry jeune poète.* Paris: Presses universitaires, 1960. A study of Valéry's early poems, not as they appear in the *Poésies,* but as they were originally published.

II. Articles on Valéry. (A highly selective list, limited mainly to recent articles.)

AUSTIN, LLOYD J. "Paul Valéry compose 'le Cimetière marin,'" *Mercure de France*, vol. 317, pp. 577–608, April, 1953; vol. 318, pp. 49–72, May, 1953. An essential study, not superseded by later books or articles.

————. "The Negative Plane Tree," *L'Esprit créateur*, IV, 1, pp. 3–10, spring 1964. Interesting discussion of "Au Platane."

————. "The Genius of Paul Valéry," *Wingspread Lectures in the Humanities:* Racine, Wisc., The Johnson Foundation, 1966, pp. 39–55. Best *brief* introduction to Valéry in English.

BÉMOL, MAURICE. "Paul Valéry, *Cahiers*, tomes I et II," *Revue d'Histoire littéraire de la France*, vol. 58, pp. 556–561, Oct.-Dec., 1958.

————. "Paul Valéry, *Cahiers*, tomes III-X," *Revue d'Histoire littéraire de la France*, vol. 60, pp. 245–259, Apr.-June, 1960. These two articles provide an excellent introduction to the *cahiers*, more thorough than the book of Madame de La Rochefoucauld.

BONNEFOY, YVES, JACQUES CHARPIER, EDOUARD GLISSANT, and JACQUES HOWLETT. "Valéry et nous," *Lettres nouvelles*, September, 1958, pp. 234–253. Three of these young poets admire Valéry; Bonnefoy has some reservations.

CHAMPIGNY, ROBERT. "The Zeno stanza," *L'Esprit créateur*, IV, 1, pp. 11–18, spring 1964. Discussion of the importance of this famous twenty-first stanza of the "Cimetière marin."

FÉLINE, PIERRE. "Souvenirs sur Paul Valéry," *Mercure de France*, vol. 321, pp. 402–428, July, 1954. Féline's reminiscences published in *Paul Valéry vivant* covered only their youthful days in Montpellier. This tells of their life-long friendship, and publishes some fifteen *lettres inédites* from Valéry to Féline.

INCE, W. N. "Composition in Valéry's writings on Monsieur Teste," *L'Esprit créateur*, IV, 1, pp. 19–27, spring 1964. Discussion of Valéry's principal problem in *Teste* and the *Lettre de Madame Teste:* how to make credible this inhuman character.

LAWLER, JAMES R. "Paul Valéry, *Cahiers*, tomes XXII-XXIX," *Revue d'Histoire littéraire de la France*, vol. 63, pp. 62–89, Jan.–Mar., 1963. Very useful analysis.

————. "The Serpent, the Tree and the Crystal," *L'Esprit créateur*, IV, 1, pp. 34–40, spring 1964. Three metaphors that recur in the *cahiers:* the serpent is knowledge or self-knowledge, the tree represents the ideal growth of meditation, the crystal is purity.

WEINBERG, BERNARD. "An interpretation of Valéry's 'Le Cimetière marin,'" *Romanic Review*, April, 1947, pp. 133–158. Simpler interpretation than that by Gustave Cohen.

Index

This lists names of persons (except Paul Valéry, which would have appeared on every page), books by Valéry (in italics) and poems and articles (in quotes). In listing alphabetically, definite and indefinite articles have been ignored: "L'Abeille" is listed under A.